Edited by Andrew Collins

This edition first published in Great Britain in 2003 by

Virgin Books
Thames Wharf Studios
Rainville Road
London W6 9HA

A catalogue record for this book is available from the British
Library

ISBN 185227 039X

Typeset by Phoenix Photosetting, Chatham, Kent
Printed and bound by William Clowes Ltd, Beccles and London

Contents

Acknowledgements

I'd like to express my sincere appreciation to Steve and Julie Pankhurst, without whom we simply wouldn't be here: apologies for taking up yet more of your valuable 'family time' and aggravating any hangovers. Long may you live in Barnet and find yourselves watching *Postman Pat* even when Amber has left the room. Stuart Slater at Virgin Books proved an urbane and visionary co-ordinator and Vanessa Daubney the quiet linchpin of this book. Thanks also to Jamie Moore, Becke Parker and Gareth Fletcher. Peace and love to all at Ebury, who had the foresight and flexibility to 'loan' their author to Virgin: Andrew and Sarah in particular, as ever. Special thanks to Jane Bradley, one of the many smiling faces of FriendsReunited, to Kate Haldane, who gives agents a good name, to Julie Quirke, my personal editor, and to Billy Bragg, for the inspiring conversation in a field in Dorset about English nostalgia. And not forgetting Mary, who told us about FriendsReunited in the first place.

Julie Pankhurst would like to dedicate this book to Hazel Mason (née Swallow), Melanie Raynor and Susan Graham, three very good school friends who each died of illnesses far too young. 'The good times we shared will never be forgotten.'

Nine Million Stories

I am married with three cats, living in Streatham, South London. I am a
freelance writer and broadcaster working extensively for the BBC. All my
family still live in Northampton and in fact both my brother's and
sister's children have been or go to Abington Vale Primary School.

It was four cats when I first registered, but that's the sort of detail you feel
compelled to go back and change, initiating the little yellow 'UPDATED' splash
to appear beside your name. As Socrates never said: the unrevised life is not
worth living.

Does anyone remember an American TV cop show from the early sixties
called *Naked City*? Set in New York? Based on a film from the forties? I don't,
but thanks to the collective race memory that allows us all to exist in one
big cultural past, I know the programme's famous sign-off line. It went:
'There are eight million stories in the naked city – this has been one of
them.'

That phrase always comes to mind when considering FriendsReunited,
except of course they have over *nine* million stories. I include mine, not
because it's especially unusual or meaningful, but because it's one of them.
It's mine. It could be yours. It could be Chris's – a vaguely remembered
schoolfriend whose mum had the first Soda Stream you'd ever seen outside
of the TV ad promising 'an endless stream of fizzy drinks'. You remember!
Chris! Freckles! Blue Gola bag! Brought one of his dad's rubber johnnies to

school and filled it with water! Apparently he now lives in Colchester, works in IT and has two beautiful daughters. Good old Chris.

L P Hartley wrote one of the most famous first lines in English literature in the prologue to his novel, *The Go-Between*: 'The past is a foreign country: they do things differently there.' Maybe they did at the turn of the century when the book's set. Maybe in 1953 when it was written. But not any more, thanks to FriendsReunited, whose nine million individual stories populate a developing republic of like-minded citizens, willing volunteers in a great big social experiment where the past is a mouse-click away and they do things similarly there.

Yes, it's a website — a website set up by two nice people in a semi-detached house — but it's more than that. FriendsReunited may have started as a beneficiary of the millennial nostalgia boom, but it's grown into something that some days threatens to engulf us all. A brand, yes — a 'superbrand' to rival eBay and Amazon — but let's not spoil the view with corporate visions of marketing potential and Internet valuation strategy tools. FriendsReunited is the warm feeling of expectation you get when you see those four, smiling faces above the logo (of whom more later); the thrill of discovering a 'NEW' or 'UPDATED' flash next to a name you recognise.

Seemingly unimportant plot developments, such as a reduced number of cats, or increased number of daughters, are the ones that tell our individual stories, and turn FriendsReunited into a compelling, 24-hour-a-day soap opera, one where very little *appears* to happen, but appearances can be deceptive. Like a soap, it never ends, providing instead a series of cliffhangers — and new characters on a regular basis.

Other mediums are forever trying to get in on the act, making claims for interactivity, but FriendsReunited is far more real than reality TV. Think: it's a soap opera with nine million subplots, and you're in it. Although, before we get to your storyline, it seems only proper that we fill in Steve and Julie's.

Stephen and Julie Pankhurst are computer programmers, but then aren't we all these days? North Londoners both, they united while working at GEC Avionics in Borehamwood. Various other companies felt the weight of their programming experience before the big decision to leave full-time employment changed their lives – and possibly yours. Julie left MFI's systems department because she was pregnant. Steve put Bovis Construction behind him in order to pursue the freelance dream. Along with Kent-born Jason Porter, 'third man' in the FriendsReunited story, he wrote 'bespoke packages' for clients and the duo eventually formed HappyGroup, under which banner they would create Internet sites. After all, everybody needs Internet sites, even people who don't realise they do.

It's tempting to see FriendsReunited as Steve and Julie's baby, but that was Amber, strictly speaking, who was actually conceived first. In fact, without knowing it, their as-yet-unborn first daughter was the inspiration. While Julie was pregnant with Amber in the summer of 1999 she had the idea for what would become the nation's favourite website, born out of the selfish desire to find some old schoolfriends and tell them about her imminent baby. She wasn't looking for a gap in the market, but she found one; the only workable website out there for getting in touch with old schoolfriends was an American one, classmates.com, established in 1996. No use whatsoever for the alumni of Cromer Road Primary School, New Barnet.

Some pregnant women have cravings for pilchard-and-jam sandwiches; Julie's was for her own Internet site. Steve was sceptical at first, as he personally had no desire to revisit his own schooldays and couldn't see the appeal. Millions of Americans, though, had registered for classmates.com and that helped change his mind. After much procrastination and hopeful enquiries of 'Wouldn't you rather I made you a pilchard-and-jam sandwich?' he wrote the program in a week, while Julie set about cataloguing UK schools – 23,000 of them to begin with, although that number has now doubled.

Registering a domain name for the new site was tricky, as pretty much every half-decent permutation featuring the word 'school' or 'class' had been taken. Looking back on it now, Steve and Julie are glad they chose 'friends' as the site has evolved into much more than a search engine for schools. It's bigger than that. But it started small.

FriendsReunited went live in July 2000. It was, as they say in the Internet biz, a 'soft launch'. In other words, quiet. As quiet as the street in Barnet where it happened without fanfare and without fireworks. Only Steve, Julie, Jason and their immediate circle of friends and relatives were registered at first, but – thanks to a lot of time spent putting the word out on message boards and other search engines – it was only a matter of days before outsiders began entering their details. The first was a man called Mike Cross (don't bother trying to find him – there are about 28 of them now). Registration grew by twos and threes at first, then fives and tens (what a thrill it was when they reached the first ten!). As originally intended, the site was working out as a happy distraction for Julie, a sideline, a hobby – certainly not a money-making exercise, or a giant go-between for a sixth of the population of Britain. The most important thing at that stage, with Steve still pursuing other Internet ideas and doing consultancy work to bring home the bacon, was that FriendsReunited was *working*. As indeed was HappyParty, the children's party-bag site run by Jason and his wife Anne.

That was July. By October, all of Steve and Julie's spare time was filled answering e-mails, improving the schools database and tweaking the site to make it more user-friendly. Already success stories were coming in from those who had tracked down old mates through the site, but it had yet to actually take over the Pankhurst family's lives.

Amber was eight months old. So was the new Millennium.

It's important to put the FriendsReunited story into context. Let's think big. Renowned economist Francis Fukuyama famously decreed in 1989 that the last days of the Cold War signalled no less than 'the end of history'. Nice try. What actually happened at the beginning of the 1990s was the *beginning* of history. When the Berlin Wall came down – when liberal, capitalist democracy was said to have 'won' – it actually gave the West a chance to chill out and reflect. You didn't have to indulge in Fukuyaman triumphalism to see that the domino-like collapse of Communism marked a turning point. And just in time too, as the end of the century, the end of the Millennium, was going to be a busy time: all those retrospective lists to make!

The past kind of caught up with us all at the end of the 1990s, the first time most of us would have seen off an entire century on New Year's Eve. A thousand years of history, in fact – from the Battle of Hastings to Bosnia – consigned to our collective outbox in the time it took to clink glasses and snog a perfect stranger. No wonder we all started to reminisce like there was no tomorrow. According to Y2K-bug Armageddon theorists, there wasn't.

In the event, New Year's Day 2000 passed off without our microwave ovens bringing Wall Street and air traffic control to a grinding halt. Indeed, it felt like just another day. Not for Steve and Julie Pankhurst, who became proud parents for the first time on that historic Saturday, but for most of us.

Nostalgia has always been with us – I expect fifteenth-century Italians used to sit around reminiscing about the 'good old days' before the Renaissance – but it seemed to infect the whole population at the end of the Millennium. Britain is the world capital of nostalgia – far more so than any other comparable European country – and this seems to be down to a mixture of island mentality and surviving the Blitz. Unlike France, we are not haunted by the spectre of occupation; unlike Germany, we have not had to rebuild our national identity to exorcise Nazism; unlike our closest cultural ally the United States, our history is not built on a bloody period of history that dare not speak its name. Our only true loss has been the Empire, but that went not with a bang but a series of handshakes and flags being lowered. Additionally, with no revolution to disrupt their lineage, the Royal Family lend a sense of continuity to all our yesterdays. All this, and you can see why British people are comfortable with the abiding notion that things ain't what they used to be.

In the year 2000, conversations about *The Clangers* and Space Dust moved from the confines of the pub to national television. That summer, taking its lead from previous experiments in self-archiving television like *TV Heaven*, *TV Hell* and *TV Offal*, BBC2 launched *I Love The 70s* – a light-hearted talking-head series that devoted an hour a week to each year of that once-unfashionable decade. It was a watershed commission and a wild sugar-rush of nostalgia not dissimilar to eating Space Dust. Countless other copycat series came flooding in its wake: *Top Tens*, *TV Years*, *Pop Years*, *The 100 Greatest* . . . remembering *The Clangers* and Space Dust had become a spectator sport. *I Love The 80s* and *90s* were not far behind, with 'yesteryear' websites like TV Cream and TV Ark flourishing. Repeats of old sitcoms became 'classic episodes' and drew millions of viewers. UK Gold launched UK Gold 2. And, for ravers of 'a certain age', SchoolDisco.com turned into the happening new club night in London.

Meanwhile history became the new rock'n'roll.

The end of the twentieth century had already seen a flush of documentaries and motion pictures devoted to the Second World War — from *The Nazis: A Warning From History* to *Saving Private Ryan* — as if perhaps the generation born after the war suddenly became aware that the generation who fought it were on their last legs. Steven Spielberg had already set up the Survivors of Shoah Visual History Foundation in 1994, devoted to simply videotaping testimonies of Holocaust eyewitnesses while they were still around. It was this kind of recording zeal that represented the end of the old century and the beginning of the new one, even if it was just a stand-up comedian recalling how much bigger Wagon Wheels were when he was a kid.

They were though, weren't they?

And it was out of this whirlwind of nostalgia — trivial and momentous — that FriendsReunited emerged and ultimately prevailed. In an era when historians like Simon Schama and David Starkey are famous enough to be impersonated on *Dead Ringers*, it's no wonder that seeking out old schoolfriends on the Internet is not just an acceptable act, it's virtually compulsory. Living in the present is *so* last year.

Whether or not the desire to reconnect with our past is a sign of something more psychologically troubling than nostalgic nosiness is one for the psychologists. Thanks in part to the endeavours of Steve, Julie and Jason, it's certainly gone way past the 'fad' stage.

Meanwhile, figures released by the Universities and Colleges Admissions Service in July 2003 showed a year-on-year rise of 4.3 per cent in students applying to study history. Books about Stalingrad and what the Victorians did for us jostle for bookshop space with grim childhood memoirs and funky novels set in the 1970s. At present, we all seem to have one foot in the past. Perhaps Fukuyama got it slightly wrong, and 1989 merely signalled the end of geography.

In December 2000, FriendsReunited underwent a facelift and a relaunch, again fairly soft. A friend of Steve's designed the new logo, which has remained unchanged ever since.

Such window dressing might have drawn comparisons with the rearrangement of deckchairs on the *Titanic*. After all, the site wasn't making a penny. The bottom had fallen out of the late-90s Internet boom early in 2000, with high-profile start-ups like lastminute.com and boo.com going under, or suffering big losses amid much talk of 'dot-bombs' and 'e-slump'. Even world-beating success story Amazon saw its share price dive by 20 per cent in June. As such, banner advertising for a modest, no-bells, no-whistles school pals site was impossible to come by. Still, the new logo looked nice.

But who are those four people who look like the Mafia on a skiing holiday? It's one of the most frequently asked questions about FriendsReunited, so for the record (from left to right): Steve's dad, Steve's mum, and the Pankhursts' friends, Dave and Jeanette. Steve's dad was taking the mickey with that rictus grin in the original photo, by the way, but now it's preserved for all time in internet amber. Steve simply supplied his designer friend with a bunch of digital snaps and she selected the famous four without knowing who they were. As soon as Steve and Julie saw it they said yes. And now it's one of the most recognisable in the country — even if most people do think Dave is a girl.

Steve has calculated that with FriendsReunited receiving between 100 and 200 million hits a month, those four faces have been seen 2–3 *billion* times on the Internet. More than any other faces in the world. Good job most of them are wearing dark glasses — they'd be mobbed if they ever stood in a line in public and Steve's dad pulled 'that face'. Some have said he looks like he's on drugs. Be assured that he is not. Others say, 'Get rid of the old people!' perhaps not realising the old people are family.

Steve and Julie are understandably loath to change the famous logo now, after all they've gone through together. It would be like scrapping the old red phone boxes or changing Opal Fruits to Starburst. It's impossible to gauge, but I think the four faces are intrinsic to FriendsReunited's success. They speak of Snappy Snaps and pulled grins, something with which we can all identify; they say 'all ages are welcome here' which is rare for the Internet; and Dave is looking over Steve's mum's shoulder in a really odd, out-of-perspective way, which means you keep looking at it. It won't win any design awards any time in the future, but it only took half an hour and life's short enough as it is.

As 2000 turned into 2001 — almost a year into the life of HappyGroup, exactly a year into the life of Amber Pankhurst and six months into the life of a popular but profitless Internet site — 3,000 people were registered with FriendsReunited. That was enough to sap a suburban family's life of its quality time and sufficient to pique the interest of the media. Internet magazine .net got in first, interviewing Steve and Julie in January and taking Julie back to the playground of Cromer Road Primary School for photographs.

On the same day, all hell broke loose. Radio 2's resident net-head, Miles Mendoza, made FriendsReunited 'Website of the Day' on Steve Wright's afternoon show and effectively shut it down in the process. The server — that is, the software package that supports or hosts the site's activity — couldn't cope with the sudden influx of new users and crashed. Steve and Jason worked through the night like surgeons trying to keep a patient alive with the Internet equivalent of a crash cart. By the end of the week, FriendsReunited had doubled its membership. By February, it was up to 19,000. Crisis point had been reached. Amber was growing up without parents. Steve and Julie were doing late-night shifts in the front room on laptops answering e-mails when they should have been doing long-forgotten things like talking to each other or watching the news. And still no money was coming in.

Worse than that, as if to confirm the site's popularity, it was now being abused, with spam — unwanted junk mail — being sent to other members via the contact e-mail system. So, after much soul-searching, they introduced the £5 charge — the price of a couple of drinks, calculated in the pub (although how they found time to go to the pub remains a mystery). It's always a risk introducing an admission fee on a website — on the one hand you have seasoned web-users who *expect* information and services to be free and feel affronted when confronted with a pound sign, on the other you have inexperienced surfers who remain nervous about inputting credit card details and sending them off into cyberspace. The solution was to charge only those members who wished to use the e-mail contact system — FriendsReunited would remain free for anyone who wanted to register their details, have a nose and log off again.

As for credit card details paranoia, Steve and Julie were inundated with envelopes containing cheques for £5 from the Internet-nervous. The bank were none too pleased. But the bank would get over it.

'What a great life it would be if we could actually make a living out of FriendsReunited!', dreamed Julie.

Well, the steady influx of cheques and credit card numbers certainly supported this fantasy. By May 2001, FriendsReunited was a national talking point. It had hit the water coolers. With membership approaching 100,000, Steve and Jason drew up a business plan – spreadsheets being a speciality – and went in search of further investment. Their projections, based on current take-up, predicted a mind-blowing one million users in five years. The figures were however slightly off. They actually reached a million in *two months*.

Malcolm Gladwell, a staff writer on *The New Yorker*, has defined moments when, almost imperceptibly, trends turn into mainstream obsessions as 'tipping points'. His book on the subject, *The Tipping Point,* is subtitled *How Little Things Can Make A Big Difference*. The Internet itself 'tipped' in 1993, when browsers began to appear, guiding surfers to other websites and stoking the explosion that followed (300 million users by the end of 1999). Gladwell, who once reported on AIDS, likens such shifts in communications and culture to the moment in an epidemic when a virus reaches critical mass, or boiling point. FriendsReunited reached its own tipping point in the summer of 2001.

Interest snowballed, thanks to exposure in the press, on radio (local and national) and TV. They hired a PR company, Beatwax, to look after the press side of things. Jason and Anne closed down HappyParty to devote themselves to FriendsReunited and, not before time, Steve and Julie began to delegate some of the e-mail-answering and database tasks to friends who needed part-time work. This was just as well, as Julie got pregnant again in July. Again, how they found the time ... let's not go there. Sally would be born in March 2002, by which time page impressions for the site (that's each time anyone clicks on one) were up to 230 million a month.

Some more numbers to lower your jaw: between August 2001 – the tipping point – and July 2002, FriendsReunited clocked up 337 pieces of national press coverage, 1,355 regional pieces and over 25 TV and 50 radio pieces. It continued to ask 'Where did you hear about FriendsReunited?' when you registered for the first time, but the question was becoming redundant.

The 'great life' Julie had wished for was a reality. A lot of technical stuff went on in the latter half of 2001, like increasing the number of servers, changing ISP (Internet service provider), doubling bandwidth — all of which simply meant everything got bigger and more efficient. E-mail traffic had got so thick (up to 4,000 a day), they hired an outside call centre to deal with it, and handed advertising queries over to an advertising agency, even though a single banner ad at the top of the site was all that was available. At this stage, FriendsReunited could have sold ad-space in Dave and Jeanette's sunglasses, but Steve and Julie were never in this for the money.

Very few people know this, but they could have sold FriendsReunited at the end of 2001. An offer was on the table. They decided against it, and employed extra hands instead.

There is an ethos to FriendsReunited (and by definition HappyGroup) that must constantly infuriate profit-oriented media partners: trust. The reason the site became a national institution in just over a year is that its members feel safe there; unexploited, unhurried and unhassled by what is still a family-run business. When you log on, you are not bombarded with 'pop-up' adverts and click-here boxes, nor are your senses assaulted with slow-to-load animations or scrolling text. In the same way that Steve and Julie have remained, well, Steve and Julie, FriendsReunited remains a reassuring constant in an ever-changing world, resisting offers of fancy redesigns and new logos. Even the first spin-off compilation CD slipped into record racks with minimal fuss and went gold anyway.

In the words of David Brent in *The Office*, 'Trust received, responsibility given.'

Steve has vowed to stand firm against unnecessary cosmetic or commercial changes and would rather die than allow intrusive advertising to infect the site. Having devoted so much of their lives to FriendsReunited during Amber's first year they were not about to allow it to be corrupted by the wrong sort of progress. They still get letters from keen potential members asking advice on which first-time PC to buy — it's that much of an incentive to the cyber-virgin. FriendsReunited is good for the home computer industry and it's good for the Internet, especially at a time when chatrooms are never far away from bad press and threatened restrictions and e-mail is accused of destroying the art of conversation.

The e-mail versus telephone debate will run and run, but in the case of FriendsReunited, there seems to be a clear winner. The once-removed protection afforded by the site's go-between role – you e-mail them; they e-mail your old friend; your old friend is under no obligation to reply – makes the site a winning advert for the advantages of electronic mail. If you even *had* the phone number of Chris with the Soda Stream, would you make that call? Or would you put if off? Not everybody gives good phone. Sending an e-mail means that you can compose your initial approach with care – wording it correctly, taking days over it if needs be – and then send it in the blink of an eye. Phoning someone you haven't spoken to for, say, 20 years, has the potential to be an awkward occasion. With the tried-and-tested FriendsReunited contact system, you can drop a casual line to anyone. If the initial flurry of correspondence goes well, *then* you might exchange phone numbers and perhaps even meet up and get married and have babies. E-mail is a safe way of making first contact.

Having said that, FriendsReunited has not been entirely free of abuse. The message boards, started as a kind of graffiti wall for ex-pupils to swap memories in public about teachers, lessons and school dinners, ran into trouble early on. Although we're not at liberty to repeat them here, certain comments were posted about certain teachers that crossed the line from light-hearted *I Love School* reminiscence into slander and libel.

In November 2001, Steve and Julie were contacted not by the aggrieved teachers themselves but by the National Union of Head Teachers, who threatened to sue FriendsReunited, if the comments weren't taken down. Sensing a backlash against the site, the message boards were swiftly taken down *en masse*, much to the chagrin of certain members, who threatened to cancel their subscription (even though you don't need to be a paid-up member to access the boards).

They remained down for a couple of months while Steve, Julie and co read every single post and removed any that might potentially cross the line. It was a miserable time for them: not only was the work dull, it meant that they weren't serving their members.

But FriendsReunited was bound to become a victim of its own success sooner or later. The teachers' threat was seen off (the boards were back up by Christmas and the site began helping to promote the Teaching Awards), but we all know that the British press prefers an unhappy ending to a happy one, and stories about marriages wrecked by the site started to come thick and fast.

You have to move quickly if you're managing a nine-million-user message exchange. As the *Observer* had it in their headline from May 2002, 'Web hath no fury like a woman scorned' – an aggrieved spouse left 'a withering, explicit and abuse-filled' message on the boards about her husband's infidelities. Worse, she posted the full address and phone number of the accused scarlet woman. Steve pulled the message within 48 hours, but it became something of an e-mail cult, as it had already been cut and pasted and entered cyberspace as that week's 'you've got to read this' attachment.

What passed as a minor incident pointed up that FriendsReunited is not all hearts and flowers. Meeting up with old flames can damage your marriage. But can what the *Observer* called 'the growing list of divorces and painful separations' really be heaped on Steve and Julie Pankhurst's doorstep? As the *Sunday Times* observed, 'Blaming a website is like citing the telephone for divorce in previous decades.'

Shirley Bell left her husband of 25 years and her three children just two weeks after making contact, via FriendsReunited, with her childhood sweetheart Steve Morgan. 'It really is like something out of a Mills & Boon novel,' he told the press. Not for the dumped husband and kids, but again, don't shoot the go-between.

As Steve insists, the site is about reuniting friends – just like it says on the tin – not about catching criminals. A cocksure gentleman registered, boasting to old schoolpals about how well he was doing – unfortunately, he chose to reveal the source of his new-found wealth: drug dealing. The police stepped in and he was put away.

Rather more seriously, police have used FriendsReunited to catch a paedophile. In June 2003, former teacher Peter Hamilton-Legget was jailed for eight years for sexually abusing schoolboys. Detectives posted a message on the site asking former pupils of a prep school in Bradford-on-Avon, Wiltshire 'Do you have anything you want to tell the police?' Nineteen came forward and the police were able to convict Mr Hamilton-Legget.

Detective Sergeant Martin called the website 'a vital tool'.

As FriendsReunited moves into its third trading year – with workplaces, regiments, teams, clubs and associations added to the schools database and add-ons like e-cards, exam re-sits and spin-offs like the family-tree finder GenesConnected and dating service FriendsReunitedDating all growing – it remains more vital than ever to many of its members. (There will always be those who, like a friend of mine, are unconvinced of its merits, and believe that member entries can be divided into two categories: Cocky and Needy, but hey, it's his democratic right to feel that way.) The membership growth curve has inevitably 'plateau-ed out', as they say, but it's still attracting up to 5,000 new members a day. And Steve has still only found two out of the six key schoolfriends he'd hoped to reunite with. It's not over yet.

To its member it's priceless, but HappyGroup found out how much FriendsReunited was actually worth in late 2002. The press pounced on the news that the site was to be sold off to the highest bidder.

Concerned that they were missing opportunities and frankly overcome by curiosity, Steve and Julie were merely casting around, testing the water, 'considering their options' – but given the choice between the truth and the legend, the press will always print the legend. According to breathless reports, the founders of the nation's favourite website had already callously flogged *your* personal details to a major supermarket – or was it a dating agency? – for £20 million ... no, £25 million ... wait a minute, £35 million! Sell! Sell! Sell!

The snide press and resultant deluge of unhappy e-mails helped convince Steve, Julie, Jason and Anne to retain control of FriendsReunited and simply hand the management side over to people who know about that kind of stuff. They hired former *Financial Times* man Michael Murphy (responsible for building FT.com) as chief executive officer of HappyGroup and Rob Mogford as chief financial officer. As I write, FriendsReunited is still FriendsReunited, Steve and Julie still live in Barnet, Amber is three and a half and Sally is one year and five months.

Which is where we leave Steve and Julie's story for now. There are nine million and this has been one of them. Now it's time for yours.

Message Boards

The message board idea is hardly unique to FriendsReunited. Many websites offer the equivalent of a visitors' book or noticeboard, a place for people to drop a line to others, ask an infrequently asked question or start a heated debate. The FriendsReunited message boards, launched in February 2003 after the ongoing popularity of individual school forums, act as a shared area where members can meet, greet and reminisce about TV, music and toys. The boards were an instant hit, and – as is the way with these things – quickly took on a life of their own. With new subjects and threads being introduced all the time, they now exist as a true online community. Sometimes discussions about the Spectrum ZX, Frank Zappa or Fuzzy Felts take the shape of a real discussion; often, the result is an impenetrable ramble among friends. Some threads reveal a 'conversation' made up of literally thousands of messages. The boards are now very much a cult and provide a snapshot of what FriendsReunited members are saying to each other throughout this book.

Though 'dodgy' comments will result in a discussion thread being dropped by mediators, as a rule no topic is off-limits. However, as you will see from this odd selection, not all of them draw a crowd.

What are you having for your tea?

Is 30 old?

Worst car owned: 1 reply

Are you boring?

Why women nag

The headmaster's office: lots of innuendo in this one

Bargain Hunt: millions of fans debate David Dickinson's 'tan' – 'definitely a sun worshipper, but he is of Armenian descent'

Regional playground: 0 replies

Why are we here?: 8 replies

David Van Day (from the eighties pop group Dollar): Queries included, 'Someone out there must know where David's famous burger van is, give us a clue... we'd love to visit him!!'

Peter Kay: popular, with 105 replies

Branston pickle and piccalilli: 0 replies

Do you read on the loo?

Mods: they are still around, many over 40

Best music to have sex to: choices included Guns N' Roses ('great'); Enrique Inglesias ('very good, I promise u') and 'Eye Of The Tiger', the theme from *Rocky*!

My Cars from '63 to '03: A David Taylor lists:

'1. In 1963, a 1949 Morris Minor.

2. In 1964, a 1955 MG ZA.

3. In 1967, a 1966 Hillman Minx

4. In 1969, a 1965 BMW 1800.

5. In 1972, a 1965 Austin Cambridge.

6. In 1973, a 1968 Triumph 2000.

7. In 1975, a 1970 Vauxhall Viva.

8. In 1977, a 1977 Vauxhall Cavalier. Moved to Canada in 1980.

9. In 1980, a 1979 Ford Mustang

10. In 1982, a 1981 VW Scirocco.

11. In 1984, a 1984 Toyota Celica.

12. In 1987 a 1987, Pontiac 6000 STE. Moved to USA in 1987.

13. In 1994, a 1994 Toyota Camry.

13a. During a six-month visit back to the UK, a Ford Scorpio Cosworth.

14. In 1996, a 1996 Lexus ES 300.

15. In 1999, a 1999 Toyota Camry.'

(Sadly, no one has replied as yet.)

I'll Be
There For You

It seems like an apposite place to start. Friendship lies, not surprisingly, at the heart of FriendsReunited. It's never really been *about* school – it's simply that school's where most alliances and acquaintances are forged. What the deluge of e-mails under this heading proved, time and again, is how easy it is to pick up where a friendship left off, years, even decades later. Time may erode coastlines, ice caps and hairlines but not friendships formed over a Bunsen burner or behind the bike sheds. Of course, when you're young, you don't always appreciate the depth or importance of your companionships – you take your mates for granted – and when school ends, or you move away, efforts to stay in touch are not always rigorous. You exchange a couple of letters and then, frankly, move on to your next friend. Which is why FriendsReunited has proved so popular, and why the following tales of often trepidatious reunification are so typical of the experience. In the words of Shalamar, 'We share the good and the bad times/Friends, ooh, ooh/Hangin' out, it's no problem/My friends, ooh, ooh.' A sentiment we can all identify with.

Not The Last Of The Summer Wine

I met up with my long lost best friend through FriendsReunited.

I met Kathryn in Class 2 at school. She had joined my school from another and I had just returned to my school after spending a year in another part of the country whilst my dad was at college. So, although I already knew everyone at the school (as I had gone to play school in the village and had completed nearly a year at the school before going away), it was as if we were both new. We bonded then and stayed friends right up until we lost touch at 18 (we are both 31 now).

When we met recently, we found it really easy to talk to each other, no awkward silences or anything. There were funny similarities. We both have confident children with really pleasant natures. We both drive old bangers and don't care. We both still smoke crafty fags. We both still start talking at the same time to say the same thing. We both have the same memories and so many of them – like the time when we were about 11 and my dad was driving us to another village to perform in a singing concert with the school's 'Entertainer's Club'. My dad was telling us about how he preferred riding his motorbike to driving a car because on his bike he could 'really feel the road'. We, being 11, thought the word 'feel' was highly amusing (as in, 'Let's have a feel of your bum/boobs [delete as appropriate]'). My dad couldn't understand what we were laughing at and said we were 'simpletons'.

The journey got even funnier when we couldn't find the place where we were supposed to be entertaining and Dad stopped to ask somebody, who, unfortunately for him, had a speech impediment (or rather, he couldn't pronounce his 'R's). When he said, 'You go up the road and it's on your right,' we collapsed in fits of giggles all over again. If you remember the TV comedy *Last of the Summer Wine*, he said it in the same way that Wally (Nora Batty's husband) would have said it.

Talking of *Last of the Summer Wine*: for our school's 10th birthday celebration in 1980, the school organised for Bill Owen (Compo) to visit the school at the summer fête, but he agreed only on the condition that we sold enough of his single 'Compo's Gone And Lost His Wellies'. Now, this single wasn't very good and we didn't sell enough copies and he pulled out. The school must have done some serious negotiating with his agent because he did turn up in the end, but he was really miserable and nobody cared about him being there. The main thing that sticks out in my mind is that I didn't even know who he was as we didn't watch *Last of the Summer Wine* at our house. I remember that when the school told us Bill Owen would be visiting, Kathryn knew who he was, I was dead impressed.

So, last year, I was browsing through the names of people who were at my first school. There she was, with two kids. I couldn't believe it. I e-mailed her straight away and told her about my little boy and my life etc. She was so pleased I had got a child as everyone else she knows hasn't even settled down yet and we have been in touch ever since.

The funny thing is that I always imagined she would end up with a really good career, but she is just like me; we both work part-time in administration roles and still have so much in common that it's like we've never been apart.

Julie Hardy, Barnsley

My Dad

My dad, Ray, doesn't use the computer very much and he certainly wouldn't think about joining up to FriendsReunited – he can be a sad man, with a lot of problems. I can remember what he used to be like when I was a little girl: fun, happy, full of life and so nice to be around.

When I found out about FriendsReunited, I thought I would join up and see how many of my old friends were on there. I signed my mum and dad up too in February, just in case they found someone they used to know. I ran through the names of the people in my dad's year at school; he didn't expect to find any of his old friends. 'No, no, no,' was the only reply I got off him as I said them aloud. Then I called out a name, and he was silent, as I turned to look at him, repeating the name again, he said, 'Yes, that was a friend of mine.'

We wrote him an e-mail and sent it off. A few minutes later I heard a sniff. Again, I turned to look at my dad; he was crying with nostalgia – the first time I have seen him cry since his mum died.

'I remember his brother throwing his cat out of the upstairs window,' he said, 'just to see if it landed on its feet.'

My dad never talks to me about his past, or his school days, and he's not very good at keeping in touch with people he knows, especially through the Internet, but he did write a reply to his friend from FriendsReunited.

A few weeks later we got a reply back to his e-mail. It explained how the friend of my father remembered my father's dad, 'I often have thoughts of you when I pass the house, I remember your dad in the mornings sat in his chair getting fresh air into his lungs'. My dad was again moved by this, but he didn't cry. He just sat there and listened as I read it out. We wrote a reply back and I think he found that quite hard. He hasn't kept in touch with anyone else from his school and he didn't contact anyone else, as we didn't find anyone.

Thanks to FriendsReunited my dad has had a chance to remember the good ol' days that he loved so much. He's had a chance to remember his friends and family and some of the things they did. And I have had a chance to see a little bit of my old dad back. I saw a part of him that I haven't seen for ages.

Gemma, Witney, Oxfordshire

Old Haunts

I tried to contact a Bob Tushingham from the FriendsReunited page but heard nothing. Then right out of the blue came an e-mail from Des Jones, a pal from over 60 years ago. He lived in Rockside Road and I was in Cooper Avenue North, both in Liverpool 18, in the late thirties and early forties. We haven't met yet, but I hope we will soon.

We both have memories of a place across the main road on which I lived from the age of five to 26, the 'Haunty'. It was a large old mansion in its own extensive grounds. It was always empty and falling down for as long as I remember – no windows, no doors etc. (In those days no one stole lead and so on.) When we kids went 'exploring', the wind would often slam one of the inside doors, or a floorboard creaked. These were always ghosts to our minds and hence it was called the 'Haunty'. During the war, the local fire-watchers used to set parts of it on fire to practise putting out fires.

They also pulled down the old tower as it was unsafe.

Ah, great days! But dangerous too.

One night, in late November 1940 at 8.00 p.m. a 2000lb bomb dropped on the grass verge between our house and the main road. The front of our house vanished but we were in the rear and were OK. The main blast from the explosion went half a mile each way along an underground stream that had been used as our sewer. That saved all our lives. The problem was that the siren hadn't sounded so the first we knew was the bang!

Sadly, there do not seem to be many from my area of my age that are on FriendsReunited, but I do have contact with quite a few old boys.

Brian Mills (now known as John), Liverpool

Reunited With Robbie

I am 49 now and I used to live in Temple Hill, Dartford. We had good neighbours and the boy next door was my first love. I was four; Robbie Walden was his name, and we went to school together, but in 1966 when we were 12 Robbie's family moved to Canada.

I remember the day very well. As the mini bus drove off down the road I was crying my eyes out, and all the family were in tears. Well, we never kept in touch – we were young. But through a friend (another neighbour) we heard that the mother had passed away and we were saddened by the news. Then, last year, I found FriendsReunited and registered myself. I found lots of schoolmates – it was so good to see those names again – but hey, the name that stood out was Robert Walden! I cried and cried. I sent an e-mail asking if he remembered me; he replied, of course. We exchanged e-mails and this year we met: he came over from Canada with his 82 year old dad, George. My own Dad was over the moon to see his old friend again.

I was initially worried — what will we talk about? — but we had no problem at all. The old memories came flooding back: how each Christmas morning we went into George's house, Dad for a whiskey, Mum for a gin and us kids for a colouring book. I loved Mrs Walden's open coal fire; she had apple trees in her garden also. We talked and talked and it was like they had never been away.

Now we're not going to lose touch again. I hope to visit Robbie in Canada one day; we plan to meet up in another ten years if not before. We had a good time. He never married — perhaps he was waiting for me!   but I am married and have been for 26 years. Sorry, Robbie!

Pamela Abbey, Dartford, Kent

Sent To Coventry

Whilst at secondary school, I was evicted from my original group of friends because I did not want to smoke. They all did. I tried, but found it repulsive, so exercised my wish not to. The girls decided because I did not conform that I should no longer be part of the group. This devastated me, but did not change my mind. I stuck to my beliefs and wishes. The girls 'sent me to Coventry' at first, then taunted me.

On the bright side, the boys found this abhorrent and in turn sent the group themselves to Coventry. They were so kind and supportive to me.

I also found new, true friends, who stood by me and me by them, no matter what. Moreover, we respected each other.

We have all moved on now, as our school was fed from very diverse areas, and we have all taken different paths. However, I have been in touch with these true friends through your website in the last year. Thank you.

Anonymous

Mad, Not Mad

I'm a relative newcomer – about six months – to PCs and FriendsReunited, and it's great!

I put myself on FriendsReunited for my old school, Chichester Boys High, 1959–1967, which is absolutely buzzing and my old Cambridge college, Sidney Sussex, 1967–1970. Apparently, I'm the only person who was there during those years. What a miserable bunch! We weren't, in fact, but I've contacted the 'Development Officer', Wendy Hedley, and we are both at a loss to understand why there is such a lack of interest.

My old teacher training college, King Alfred's, Winchester, has a modest show of interest, but best of all is Thornden School, Chandler's Ford, where I taught from 1979 to 1993. I have enlisted as an ex-'pupil', which gives me access to all the 'teacher memories' about me. Some revelations there!

Or maybe not.

I'm mainly remembered as nice but mad. What an accolade! The abiding image is of Roger, the toy chimpanzee, who was given to me by my tutor group and who I 'kept' for five years – the whole of their secondary schooling. Under a bizarrely liberal system, we were allowed to elect, or reject, our tutor groups on grounds of compatibility. New teachers tended to be 'lumbered' with a first-year tutor group, because John Sherbourne, the Head of First Year, was regarded as a bit of a tyrant who expected his tutors to 'do things' with their flocks: quizzes, spelling games, lectures etc. Tutors of older groups preferred to ignore their flocks whilst using the time to get ready for the day.

At the end of my first year, John Sherbourne asked me if I wanted to 'take my lot on'. I said no. It wasn't that we hated each other; I just felt there wasn't enough basis for a marriage. So John heaved a sigh of relief and said, 'You'll have another dose of first years then.' As soon as I saw the second lot, I knew: these were the ones. And we went the whole five years together.

Unbeknown to me, the Albatross house head, Dennis 'Dag' Phillips (sadly deceased and fondly remembered by myself and others in the pages of FriendsReunited) groomed two of my girls, Vicki Cummins and Jenny Rossiter, to be unofficial form captains (we didn't have those offices) and look after me when times weren't always easy. And it was Vicki who presented me, on 'our' very last day in July 1985, with the toy chimpanzee.

I called him Roger because Roger Rowland was the only person in the tutor group that it was difficult to like. He had an unfortunate background. His father taught art in one of the neighbouring schools. Art teachers always seemed to be a bit of a breed apart, though that's what my 'colleagues' thought about me.

I adored Roger because of what he represented, but ironically no subsequent pupils could ever have any inkling of that. They just thought I was a raving lunatic, who doted on a toy chimpanzee. Eventually, I gave him to a charity shop – I think it was Scope in Portswood – and I pray that some sad and lonely gypsy girl in Romania is enjoying the vicarious love of Roger the chimpanzee. He had these sticking-out arms that seemed to say 'Love me! Love me!'

Ralph Lane, Southampton.

They Call It Puppy Love

Back in 1974, my friend June Menhenett and I (both aged only 13) travelled by train from Bristol to London to see the Osmonds. We managed to persuade our parents to let us go on our own as we would be staying with my brother's fiancée's parents. However, on the day we were left to our own devices and caught the tube all over the place, including going to see the Osmonds wave from the balcony of their hotel room!

We swooned over Donny throughout the concert and June even managed to jump on his limousine to see his smiling face – she managed to crack a bone in her ankle doing this, but didn't care!

We lost touch at 16, when June left school, but thanks to FriendsReunited, June contacted me last year. She was going to see Donny Osmond in Cardiff and asked if I would like to go.

Well, of course, I did and what a great time we had. It was a really strange feeling seeing Donny all these years later and an even stranger experience having June sat next to me as she did all those years ago.

Anyway, we swooned over Donny again and it was like I had only seen June yesterday. What was really bizarre was that Donny was shown on a big screen singing a song from the concert we had been to, but this time he sang along with it!

The arena was packed and loads of women in their forties were there screaming like mad, just like the old days – they were probably there at the concert in Earl's Court too (the ones we spoke to had been!).

Carol Baker

The Last Time

I wandered onto the FriendsReunited site, about two years ago, just looking at first, checking who was there, interested in what they were doing now. Then later I added a few words about myself. I went to school in Wales and now I live in Bristol, so I had not been in touch with any of those names since my childhood. My next thought was, 'I wonder if any of them would like to hear from me?'

Before I had chance to act on this, I had an e-mail from Josie, who was my childhood friend: we played together, went to our first disco together, shared a lot of memories; then life intervened and we lost touch. She had seen my name appear on FriendsReunited. She loved her computer, and there was nothing she didn't know about them. I was so happy to hear from her, we e-mailed every week from then on, and met up, with another friend who was visiting from Australia.

I'll always remember that day — lunch in the village inn then a spur-of-the-moment visit to our old primary school, which was just next door. Over the next few months Josie and I shared what had been happening in our lives, and became very close again. She was there beside me at my father's funeral, very caring, always thought of others before herself. She had not had good health, and was very used to hospital visits, but had the patience, strength and determination of a saint.

In April she was diagnosed with leukaemia. As she couldn't access her computer at that time I wrote her a letter, and she rang to thank me — letters were such a novelty for her! She was so brave, and still fighting for her health. A few days later, at home, Josie died.

I had thought that she was back forever. I was wrong. It was such a short time that we were back in touch, but I am so grateful for the opportunity to have known her again, so I wanted to thank FriendsReunited for making it possible.

Ann Horne, Bristol

Eightysomething

A little over a year ago, I looked for my old school, Lady Edridge Grammar School, via FriendsReunited. When I found it, to my absolute amazement, there were the names of two old girls trying to contact others. These were my two best friends at school. The three of us were inseparable!

I think you will be amazed also when I tell you that we all left school in 1937 and have not seen each other since 1939. We are now in our 82nd year, have each acquired computers and have been teaching ourselves to use them.

Since our last get together a lifetime has passed – marriage, children, grandchildren and great grandchildren. We are now miles apart: I emigrated to Canada in 1965 and live in Toronto, the other two are still in England, one in York and the other in Essex.

My heartfelt wish is that we could all meet up again after all these years, although since I am unable to travel because of health problems this is extremely unlikely to happen. However, I am sure you will agree that the fact that we are still alive and are still able to function mentally to make use of the wonderful technology of this day and age is truly amazing.

I hope you will find this of interest and realise what a wonderful tribute this is to FriendsReunited.

Eileen Stevens, Toronto

Northern Soulmates

I found my best friend's name the first day I joined FriendsReunited: Susan Parkin from John Bright Grammar School in Llandudno, Wales. We both lived in Penmaenmawr and knew each other for a few years in the late sixties before losing touch when she moved to Sheffield. I now live in Leeds and she lives in

Wakefield, a mere stone's throw away – amazing. We now meet once a month in town for lunch and haven't run out of things to say.

After e-mailing Susan via the FriendsReunited website, we spoke to each other on the telephone, both of us really nervous and afraid that we would have nothing to talk about after all this time, but we spoke for over an hour that first time over the phone. I also e-mailed a photo of myself and my husband on holiday, so she had some idea of what I now looked like – now wearing glasses and a few (a lot) of pounds of extra weight since we last saw each other!

We agreed to meet in Leeds one lunchtime and I said I would be at a corner of Albion Street and The Headrow at 12.30 p.m. I arrived at the corner and waited, and waited – then I walked around the block in case I bumped into her coming out of the car park – not knowing what she now looked like didn't help either.

Just after 1.00 p.m. I heard my name being called. I saw this tall blonde running towards me with an embarrassed look on her face and knew it was her instantly. She had been looking for a parking place and had parked across the street and unbeknown to me she had been yelling my name for ages to tell me she wouldn't be long; everyone else heard her except me! This more than broke the ice and we easily fell into the old way of chatting and filling each other in on what we had been up to. I have to say that Susan has hardly changed, whilst I know I have.

At school, I don't think we had any idea of what the future held, except getting through exams and going on to marry the boy of our dreams and raise a family – normal girly stuff for the late sixties. I think everyone has certain friends who you can catch up with maybe once or twice a year and carry on the conversation from the last time as if it were yesterday. Meeting Susan again was just like that, regardless of the intervening thirty-plus years. It was as if we hadn't aged at all inside, only visibly.

As for 'the old days', I have fond memories of school, but have to say I wasn't *that* fond of it, except the social aspect, of course. We tended to live from Saturday to Saturday – weekly outings to Paynes Café in Llandudno, the disco where everyone used to meet up full of Tamla Motown, imported soul and, of course, Northern soul. We would spend the lunchtimes each week practising the latest dances so as not to look a fool on Saturday night and hope to chat up whomever it was we fancied at the time. I remember most of our boyfriends were 'really cool' in today's terms and by association so were we – or so we thought. I have a black-and-white photo, e-mailed to me by Susan's daughter, of us aged 16 at Paynes, me in my silver-blue, halter-neck dress and Susan (all glam) in maroon suede boots and skirt and top posing seriously for the camera. Hard to believe we were ever that young.

I think time has been kind to us, neither of us look as old as I expected us to. When you are 16, to be 30 is to be old and married and past it. Happily to say, I came through that age in one piece too.

I always thought that Susan would end up as a model, or at least married to a millionaire – she had such poise as well as beauty, and of course long blonde hair! Last I heard was that she was seeing someone called Phil and it looked serious. Seems it was, as she is now married to him.

Since then, we have found a pub where we meet every time. We still find things to talk about the past, as well as the present and future. It's funny that I can remember some things that Susan can't and vice versa, so we help each other fill in the gaps. There are no awkward silences, or pauses; we find ourselves running out of time before we run out of things to say. I'm really grateful to FriendsReunited for putting us back in touch, realising that we had missed each other without knowing it until now.

Susan Peat (née Beckett), Leeds

New Life

I emigrated to New Zealand in 1970 (33 years ago) and very rapidly lost contact with the majority of friends I went to school with. In August 2002 I came across the FRU site. After keying in the year I left school, I saw names I'd all but forgotten. One name stood out though: a really good mate with whom I'd lost touch. I'd treated him very badly just prior to leaving for New Zealand, and we'd never 'made up'. It had always been on my conscience, and I wished I hadn't been so stupid and that it would have played out differently. One makes a lot of acquaintances as one goes through life, but very few really good friends.

Initially I was very sceptical of the site, but I realised that the benefits could be enormous. I've now made contact with 21 people I either grew up with or went to school with, and it's been such a success that we're soon to have a reunion as I'm visiting England for the first time in 25 years. The intervening years have been swept away as though they didn't exist; all my bad actions have been forgiven, and I've now got friends I never dreamed I would ever see again. FriendsReunited has been the catalyst behind reconnecting me with my friends, and getting us all together for our 37th reunion – the last 36 of which, we've all missed! – and I can never thank them enough for making that possible.

Steve Lillyston, Greytown, New Zealand

The Accused

I was surprised to get a message from a former classmate which read, 'Are you the same person who was in Class 1A who threw a chair through the window?' This referred back to when I was aged 12 (56 years ago) and I have no such recollection, though it sounded just like the kind of mischief I *might* have got up to, possibly for a 'dare' – but I'm sure it would have been an *open* window, and I'm sure the teacher would not have been present at the time.

The classmate e-mailed from Canada and since then we have, over the past year, become e-mail pals. My family thought it was hilarious, especially my teenage grandchildren. Luckily, I have led a blameless life since and did not graduate to wrecking phone boxes or mugging old ladies!

Eileen Haworth

For Samantha

It was with one real intention that I logged on to your website: to see if I could track down my best friend from primary school, Samantha McNamee.

Within a fortnight I had a surprise announcement informing me that someone was trying to contact me. It was Samantha and it was 1 March 2002. I felt both completely amazed and delighted and wished her a happy St David's Day. We sent one another a few e-mails after that to try and catch up after a complete silence of 17 years. I was amazed by some of our similarities – the fact that we had both gone into the field of education, spoke Spanish and travelled abroad as part of our chosen career paths.

She mentioned that she would be coming over to Pembrokeshire from Mexico on holiday with her family and that it was not very far away from where I live in Wales. Unfortunately, this reunion did not take place and she died later that year in September from cancer, shortly after celebrating her 35th birthday. My joy of expectancy changed into great sadness and shock. I feel that destiny had a part in this reunion.

If you choose to publish this account of my one poignant experience, then please can it be dedicated to her, as she inspired me as a child to read, love, laugh and now ultimately to write this.

Maria Sidoli, Wales

The website may be predicated on the existence of friends who are, by their nature, flesh and blood – but that's not to say that 'imaginary friends', even ghosts, don't come up too. This particular topic caused a flurry of interest on the boards, especially in relation to childhood.

'It's amazing how many younger people seem to be "tuned in" to supernatural experiences. As a child I swear that I could see things which my siblings and parents could not see, but at the age of about five these stopped, I therefore ask, "Are imaginary friends so imaginary?" Is there credibility in my theory? Your experiences, or logic, please?'

'I wonder if imaginary friends are ghosts. I had one called Trevor. My mum said I used to get very upset when Trevor was "ill" and it all seemed so very real. I can't remember any of it now.'

'When my son was about four or five, he was talking one day about the colour around the top of a neighbour's head. I asked him what he meant and he got annoyed with me that I could ask anything so stupid. "You know, the colour that people have round their bodies." I had to explain to him that other people couldn't see it. Was he seeing auras around people? I'll never know because by the time he was about six he couldn't see it any more and he can't remember it now.'

'My son's "friend" when he was small was called Digby. He was with us for about a year and I even used to have to set a place at the table for him so he could eat with us.'

'My son (now ten) had one of these imaginary friends for quite a while when he was younger. It got so scary that I actually took him to the doctor, who just said that it was a sign of intelligence! Then, out of the blue, he just said one day that Combi (his friend's name) had gone on holiday and he never mentioned it again.'

A Family Affair

You can choose your friends, but you're stuck with your family. Have a few friends round, it's a dinner party; have the family round, it's an ordeal. Worse, it's Boxing Day. These are the truisms, but it doesn't have to be this way. Not all families that play together stay together. For all sorts of reasons families are often rent asunder, separated by miles or years, by divorce or wartime. FriendsReunited has been able to facilitate a number of serious family reunions through its search database. Natural parents have been tracked down, long-lost brothers and sisters, even family members who never knew the other existed. Family reunions can be tough: it's not like meeting up with an old school friend and wondering if you'll still get on – reconnecting with a blood relative, especially after a long period, can be awkward, disappointing, even unsuccessful and remote. But when bonding or rebonding occurs. . . needless to say, these are the stories that bring a lump to the throat, the kind that shine a good light on the often blighted Internet. Sure, it fills your inbox with spam about herbal Viagra, but it also does this.

My Life Story

I was born in 1947, in a small town in the heart of Ireland. My dad was a soldier, Mum was a singer/dancer (working with all the 'mainliners' of the time, including Ruby Murray, Joc Lynch, and The Bachelors). Mum was 17 years old when she became pregnant and was married a couple of months after. I am the eldest of the surviving seven children, and was 'Mother's Little Helper' throughout my childhood and teenage years.

We were 'Army kids', living and growing up in a variety of married quarters at several barracks. By the time I was nine years old, we had moved three times. The last move was to the West Coast of Ireland. It was, and still is, a highly traditional area, where Irish is the main language. All school subjects were taught in Irish, and we were forbidden to speak or write in English in school. This was highly distressing for us, since we had only learnt Irish as a subject in our previous schools; I was isolated and taunted by the nuns and other pupils and I withdrew into myself and totally despaired. My home life was already very stressful, as my parents had a highly volatile relationship. They both enjoyed drinking and would argue after their nights out. Mum would usually end up being hurt and bruised the next morning. I would keep the other kids quiet so that my dad would not focus his anger on us.

After falling in love with a Chinese man, I married him. It was against my father's wishes (although my mother was always supportive) and I had to handle various forms of racial abuse from former friends and locals.

I had two beautiful sons, but then I found out my husband already had a wife back in Hong Kong. He left with my two sons, leaving me homeless and jobless. I had no other option but to give up my children: life would have been too difficult for us if I had brought them up here on my own.

Two weeks later, I was in London and found work, ending up as a relief manager travelling around a variety of pubs in London. My life was hectic, which suited my need to keep occupied. I went to Liverpool to cover the manager's annual leave and I loved it there. The people were so friendly and there was a huge 'Irish' community.

Whilst I was there, I met a really great guy. We had a lot of great times, but his family was against the relationship. And my instincts told me that it would never work out, but I then found out that I was pregnant. I was absolutely over the moon, and felt really happy at the prospect of being a mum again. I told the dad, who wanted us to be married, but I had decided to go it alone.

My wonderful daughter was born in London in mid June 1972, weighing in at 9lbs 7oz. I was so happy.

I had been allocated an amazing social worker, who really helped us. She put me in touch with 'Patchwork Community' in Kingston, Surrey. It was a charity that helped homeless people, providing rooms within group houses. I became involved in the work that Patchwork did and found that I could relate to and help those around me in the Community.

I became an Area Rep for Patchwork. I loved being there and feeling part of something very special. One day, in 1980, I picked up a copy of the *Guardian* left on the bar, and looked through the job section. Barnardo's were advertising for residential staff at various locations. At first I thought that I would not stand a chance without any qualifications. However, I decided to apply. I heard nothing for weeks and had given up on the whole idea, until I received a call from Barnardo's Highclose School, in Wokingham. I was so surprised to be invited for an interview.

The school was like a 'village' within its own grounds; it was an all-girls school and had a really warm and caring atmosphere. My interview went well; the headmistress was a formidable lady. On my application form, I stated that I was a single parent and had a daughter aged eight years old and I expected this to be a problem, but weeks later I got a phone call from Highclose offering me the job! I was over the moon. I had a start date for January '81. I could have my daughter with me; they would provide accommodation for both of us.

The headmistress immediately put me on a training course, determined to 'harness' my abilities and turn me into a professional. The work with the girls was really challenging. Some had suffered severe sexual, physical, emotional and psychological abuse. I found their ability to cope quite remarkable. Their behaviour was often outrageous – mostly to test staff. They trusted nobody, and would act out their pain.

I was able to reach out to the most angry and disturbed girls who often abused themselves, ran away, overdosed, or became violent. I could engage them, and build good relationships based on mutual trust. They would disclose their abuse to me and work with me towards 'taking back control of their lives'.

There were dozens of girls in my care over the seven years I worked at Barnardo's. All of them sexually abused. Some were acute cases, for example, one girl had found out that she was born of incest where her grandfather had raped his daughter. This girl had grown up believing that her mother was her sister, until it all came out. By this time, her mother was in prison. The girl had wondered why she had been rejected and put into care by her family and why they shunned her all through her childhood. We lost touch, but I would love to hear from her.

Some girls were 'frozen' emotionally and refused to talk about what happened to them; others would attack staff who tried to control them. I was frequently called out to deal with 'difficult' girls, often deeply distressed, and obviously in a lot of emotional pain. I am still in contact with some of them.

There is one girl who sticks in my mind. She was the daughter of a prestigious family, who treated her really badly. She was kept hidden and out of the way because of her appearance and slight learning disabilities. Her parents and sister found her an embarrassment. Her sister was blonde and beautiful, while she was plain and had a skin problem. This girl was so friendly and craved affection. She loved helping staff and was very able. It was so sad that she lived such an isolated and disaffected life. She rarely went on home visits, only when the school closed for holidays, and she was so happy to return to the unit because she saw us as her family. All she wanted was to be loved and appreciated, but she was never loved nor appreciated by her own family.

When she went home, she lived in a small flat over the stables and not with the rest of the family. She cared for the horses which she loved doing, and had little involvement in the family's social life. The last I heard from her, she was still living in the flat over the stables and still being treated as a servant. The real 'Cinderella' in every sense. I often think of her, and wonder how she is?·

For many girls, when they had to leave the school that had been their home for several years, this was yet another rejection. As soon as they reached 16, they were above school age, and legally would have either to return to their families, or go into some form of hostel or assisted housing. Many were still trying to cope with their problems and needed to be safe.

My objective was to earn their trust and respect. The ethos within the unit enabled these damaged, and sometimes damaging, girls to 'act out' their rage and anger in a safe and controlled environment. One of my nicknames was 'Dragon Queen' and they often gave me awards that they would make in metalwork, such as 'Bitch Of The Year Award'. I still have these and all those very precious pieces of art.

While my years at Barnardo's were some of the toughest of my life, they were also the most rewarding. I was able to use my own experience of betrayal, rejection, loss and despair in my work. It was a mutually healing experience, and I would do it all again. I am blessed to have had such a rich life, and I now know that I was successful in helping many young women to overcome their previous self-abusive/destructive behaviours, and move on as young adults.

FriendsReunited has enabled me to regain contact with a number of the girls that I worked with at the school and the unit. Talking with them has been so amazing. They are able to express their views about my effect on their lives. How the years at the school were the best times of their lives. They recall what 'madams' they were and ask how I ever put up with them? They talk about their problems and concerns about their own children. I try to advise them on how to deal with issues. As time passes, I hear from more old girls and find out how they are doing. Some have visited me with their kids. Many keep in regular contact by e-mail and telephone. It has given me answers to so many questions, and put my mind at ease about these young women.

We are trying to organise a reunion of as many 'old girls' as possible. It would never have been possible without FriendsReunited. I have made contact with some very interesting people, and enjoy spending time on the website.

And my sons? I decided that I would try to find them in 1998, when my grandchildren were born, if only to know that they were alive and OK. I put a search on a site that concentrates on Asia, since I believed that my sons were living in Hong Kong. I heard nothing at all.

In October last year, my sister in Ireland rang me to say that a letter had arrived at her home (which was the family home), from a lady who is a friend of my eldest son. She was trying to find out my whereabouts, stating that my son wanted to find me. I was in total shock. I spoke to her within the hour She said she was happy to have found me and that she would call my son and tell him.

I sobbed and was unable to stop for hours. I really could not believe what was happening. My son rang me around 7.00 p.m. that evening. It was the most incredible feeling hearing him say 'Hello Mum'. We talked for over an hour and it turned out that both of my sons had grown up in Yorkshire! They went to Hong Kong after they left me, but only stayed a couple of years, before returning to the UK. I was devastated: they had been in the UK all those years, whilst I had believed that they were in Asia!

My son visited me in November. We met him at Reading Station. I was really nervous, so was he. I recognised him as he came down the escalator. We hugged and kissed. It felt so fantastic, after 33 years of wondering and wishing, to meet my first born son. We spent 24 hours together, and he met his sister and twin nephews. It was like a dream come true. He brought his wedding album and photos of my beautiful little three-year-old granddaughter. I had prepared two photo-albums for him of my family and of his dad and I. He had never seen any photos of himself as a baby.

His dad had initially denied my existence, but when my sons wanted their birth certificates to get passports, the game was up really, and they then found out the truth. Even then, their dad's only comment was, 'Don't forget who raised you.'

New Year was the most incredible time of my life. Both my sons plotted just to turn up to surprise me. My husband and daughter felt it would be too much, as I was still 'reeling' with it all. So my eldest son, his wife and my granddaughter arrived on New Year's Eve. I was so happy, I was just dishing up dinner when the doorbell rang. I turned around and my youngest son and his fiancée were standing behind me — the first time we had met in 33 years. I cannot describe how I felt that night, to have my three kids and three grandkids together for the very first time. What a New Year! My life was now complete, all the heartache and emotional turmoil was over; no missing pieces. I have my sons back in my life.

I am trying to consolidate my life, to merge the person who somehow coped with my two sons being taken away and the person that now exists. It's hard to look at my sons, having never had the chance to care for and love them as kids. I really am at a loss when it comes to knowing 'how to be' with them. Perhaps the part of me that died in 1970, watching my sons leave, will never come to life again. But I am now able to face each day without that awful deep 'inner pain' and sense of guilt that I have lived with for 33 years. I am now looking for a new job in childcare. It will be a new chapter in my life, this time as a complete and focused person.

Bernie Trewern, Wokingham, Berkshire

A Voyage Around My Father

I am now 20 years old and only ever saw my father once, which was when I was only a few weeks old. My parents were not married and had split up before I was born. I have moved around quite a lot with my mother and sister and two brothers, whom my mother had with a different man from whom she has now split. I am now living in South Wales, which is a rather long way from where I was born!

My mother kept no photos of my father and so I have always been curious as to what he looks like, especially as my mother often tells me I look like him. I get my height from him too as I am 5' 9", while my mother is only 5' 1"!

I guessed he would now have a new family and, although I didn't want to cause any problems for him, I really felt I had the right to find out what he's like as a person. I tried Directory Enquiries and a few other websites, but I had never heard of FriendsReunited. It was just before Christmas last year when someone at work told me about it. We put in my father's name and it brought his details up immediately – there are a few with the same name as him, but I knew which one he was from the school he went to.

Then I had to decide whether I should make contact or not – my brothers and sister had the chance to know their father, so I felt I deserved that chance too. I was concerned that he might ignore me, tell me I had got the wrong person, or even that he would say my mother was lying about him being my dad! Eventually, I decided to go ahead, but didn't really know what to say! I e-mailed him just basically explaining who I was (my surname has changed since birth). I told him I didn't want to cause problems for him and his family, but I would just appreciate getting to know a bit about him. It was a while before I had a response. He explained in his first letter that it was understandably a total shock after all these years, but he said he was OK with it and that he didn't mind if I got in touch with him again. He told me a bit about himself, but said he wasn't sure what sort of things I wanted to know so he didn't go on too much.

I have since e-mailed him about another three or four times and each time I have had another letter back. I have had three letters from him so far and am waiting for a response to my last e-mail, which I have to admit was rather long, so I just hope I haven't bored him too much! I have had so many things to ask him and, in my most recent e-mail, I have asked him if he would consider sending me a photo of himself. I really hope he does, but I will understand if he doesn't want to yet, as he is probably still slightly wary and doesn't want any complications with his new family, who don't know about me.

I just hope he does believe me when I say I'm not out to cause problems. I'm just extremely curious as to what he's like. He sounds like a lovely person, who dotes on his two children, so I hope he continues to give me the chance to find out what he's like – so far, I think he's great!

The weirdest thing is I received his first letter just a few days before I moved from that address so had he been a couple of days late, I might never have got to know anything about him. I would just like to say thanks to everyone at FriendsReunited for giving me the chance to get to know him!

Alexa Kingston

Baby It's You

I will try to make it as brief as I can, in the hope that it will be an inspiration to those who must never give up hope.

Forty years ago, for various reasons, I had my baby son of six weeks adopted. The main reason I guess was that, although I was 20 years of age, and in a long-term relationship, the father did not want to get married, though he was prepared to 'take care of us.' I would have had to live at home, with my mother and sister (having lost my father at three years of age). I didn't want them to go to work to 'take care of us', so really had no alternative but to put myself into a mother and baby home, and after the birth of Stephen, it was arranged for him to be adopted.

I did request, and receive, a photo of him when he was three months old (just prior to the official adoption), and that was it.

Years rolled by, and although he was never forgotten, it did become a little easier when I married and had another son and a daughter. Of course every birthday I did say a happy birthday to Stephen.

The latter part of 2001, because various girls in the office had joined FriendsReunited, I did also, with the idea of tracking some of my old school friends ... or was it?!

One Monday morning, 11 February 2002, I arrived in the office, opened my e-mails, and saw one from FriendsReunited. It read: 'If you are who I think you are, then this day will be as special for you as it is for me.' The name of the sender I didn't recognise and promptly replied back: 'Who do you think I am?'

For best part of that morning I kept thinking about this message, and a couple of times went back to re-read it. I looked at the date it was sent and saw Sunday, 10 February. I immediately realised it was Stephen's birthday that day, and because I had been incredibly busy, for the first time ever, I had forgotten to say happy birthday. Bells started ringing quite loudly now, and I scrutinised the e-mail, hoping for a definite clue. There at the very bottom, under his name, were the initials 'SJI'. His adopted parents had given him a completely different name (David). I then realised what the 'special' meant. He was in fact 40 on that Sunday.

Well after several e-mails, and eventually a telephone call, I did meet him, and his wife. They told me that it had taken 20 years to find me, and because of a very distinctive maiden name, they'd found me on FriendsReunited. He, his wife and two children have met with my son, daughter and husband. Now we are all aware of each other, and I have to say both my sons get on remarkably well, and have almost identical interests.

In fact my second son has many friends in the area where 'David' lives, and believe it or not, many of these friends are known by both boys. Their paths had crossed several times, but of course they were totally unaware that they were half brothers.

All David ever wanted was to know where I lived and that at any time he could call in. His dream – and mine – has now come true.

Carole Carn

Passage To India

I had taken my mock exams in 1979. At the end of the year, I was told by my dad that I would be accompanying him to Singapore to meet my grandma, who was ill. I was overjoyed at the prospect of visiting Singapore, my birthplace, and also seeing my nan and maternal uncles, whom I had never seen since I came to the UK in 1966. It was not until we reached Delhi that I was told we would be stopping over at my aunt's home in a village in Punjab for a week before continuing on our journey to Singapore. Fair enough, I thought, it would be a pleasant stay as the weather was OK and it had been a while since I had been in India.

However, I was in for a shock, when I was told that I was to stay in India and my dad would go back to the UK in a couple of weeks. When I questioned him about my going to Singapore, he said, 'This is your Singapore. This is where you will stay until I call you back!' I was devastated! Just before my dad returned to England, he instructed me to be good and learn some cooking and needlework etc. I suppose they were the only qualities he thought necessary in a good Indian wife!

I felt betrayed and humiliated. I mean, who would you trust more than your own parents?

Then I realised that I was being put through this because I did not have a mother. My mum died when I was nine years old and my dad re-married two years later. I never really got on with my step-mother, or should I say she never got on with me. I felt that she never wanted me around. All she wanted was her husband to herself and be father to her kids only! I discovered later on that it was her scheming and plotting that resulted in my being packed off to India.

Anyway, a year passed by and I heard nothing from my dad. Then one day, his uncle (my great uncle) came to my aunt's house to take me away to stay with him and his wife in a town house. They had convinced my dad that it was difficult for a kid who had been born and brought up in a western country to live in a village in India.

I went to stay with the elderly couple. They were very loving and kind towards me, until one day I met someone.

He was the son of a family friend of theirs. We started meeting secretly, as daughters of respectable families were not expected to have love affairs in those days. My great uncle found out and sent me straight back to the village in Punjab! My boyfriend found out my whereabouts and with the backing of his family came for me. To cut a long story short, we eloped to his maternal uncle's village where his parents arrived two days later with all the essential things for a wedding. We had a quiet wedding in a temple and a registered marriage later.

I had a great life there, but deep down inside I always wanted to relocate to England. Now, with my kids in their teens, I have managed to convince my husband that they would have better career opportunities in England and, so, here I am!

I have always missed my teenage years and never really got to enjoy my friends. Hopefully, FriendsReunited is a means of getting to know the ones that I have lost contact with.

Surinder

Dedication

FriendsReunited helped me locate my brother Dave.

My mother had a relationship with someone in 1969 of which I was the result. She married another man when I was seven months of age and I was brought up believing him to be my father. When I was 15, I found out the truth and had wondered about my 'other family' since then.

In 2001, I decided that I needed to discover my real roots and started on a search, which led me to my natural father's brother in Australia. He told me that my father had got married in either 1969, or 1970, and had had a family with his new wife. He believed the first child had been a boy and they named him David – he thought he'd been born in 1970, or 1971, in Colchester.

From this information, I obtained a copy of his birth certificate and established his date of birth as 12.4.71 and full name David Latham

Every week from the October of 2001 until the next February, I ran a name search on FriendsReunited to find him. In January 2002, he registered and on 17 February I e-mailed him.

The next day (my thirty-second birthday), I got a reply. It was my brother. He didn't know he had a sister and couldn't remember much about his father (last seen in South Africa in the mid seventies). We have since met and enjoyed our new-found relationship. When Dave and I met, it was very, very emotional. We were both so nervous to start with, but it felt so natural to be together – we got on so well.

So thank you FriendsReunited.

The icing on the cake was that although we both were aware that we had an older brother called Steven – born of our father's first marriage – neither of us knew more than his name. I have since located him and we have all been abandoned by our biological father – but the best thing is we all have each other.

Sharon Mooney, Colchester, Essex

Mighty Real

My good fortune through FriendsReunited was to find my 'real mum'. Once I had looked into my adoption details and had my mum's birth certificate I was able to put her maiden name, Wendy Head, into the 'name search' facility. After finding out I had a half brother and sister, I was able to determine from the details which one of the many Wendy Heads listed could be my mum.

I sent an e-mail asking did she ever live at a certain address (the one on my original birth certificate) and I was so lucky to receive a reply within the week confirming that the Wendy Head I had contacted was in fact my 'real mum'.

She had been desperate to find me but was unsure of my adopted surname. When she received my e-mail she knew it must be me as a condition of the adoption was that my name remain Caroline Jane – the name she had called me when I was born. Mum was absolutely thrilled as she had been trying to contact me for years.

I have just celebrated my 45th birthday and for the first time was able to celebrate with my 'real mum', my half brother and sister and all my new relatives. I cannot tell you how happy both I and my mum are, and it's all thanks to FriendsReunited.

Caroline Coombes

Doing It For The Kids

My husband lost contact with his three children from his first marriage, even though they all live within the same region.

Last January we decided to invest in a PC, as our bush Internet did not give us much control, and as soon as we got going, I put in my new e-mail address on FriendsReunited.

Within a week of being online I had an e-mail for my husband saying it was his eldest boy and they had been looking for him and both his other kids wanted to see him.

In this e-mail we also found out my husband was going to be a grandad.

Since then, we have all become very close and Lauren is now six months old and lovely. As for me and hubbie, I have just found out I am pregnant, so Clive's children will have another brother or sister!

Lisa Burman, Hopton, nr Great Yarmouth, Norfolk

The Lost Boy

I gave birth to David on 1 March 1968. Unfortunately, I had lost my mother in the October of the previous year, and my dad told me it would be impossible for me to keep David, as we just wouldn't be able to manage to bring him up. We all had to go to work, and there would have been nobody to look after him. I must admit it broke my heart, but I wanted him to have all the things I knew I wouldn't be able to give him.

I tried for years to find him, but just kept coming up against brick walls. I even contacted the Salvation Army to see if they could help, but they told me they couldn't get involved because it had all been handled legally through the Adoption Society and legal papers had been signed.

At work, everybody was talking about the FriendsReunited site and urged me to become a member, which I did. My husband, Reg, kept telling me not to give up trying to find David. Even though he was not the father, he was just as eager for me to find him as I was myself. Every day I went into work and checked my e-mail, but nothing. I had belonged to FriendsReunited for about three to four months, and then one morning in November 2001, I had an e-mail (through FriendsReunited) from a David Chandler.

It said, 'Are you the person that lived in Wickham Lane 34 years ago? If so, it would mean the world to me if you got back to me; if not, sorry to bother you.' Well, I'm sure my heart stopped. I just sat staring at the screen. The name Chandler didn't mean anything to me, but the name David kept jumping out from the screen at me. 'Could this really be him?' I kept thinking. My friends all said 'Go on Dot, you've got to reply!' So I did. Within no time at all I had a reply: 'I was born David Ian Mayhew, on 1 March 1968'. It was him!

I rang my husband and told him, and he told me to write back and ask for some kind of proof, as you hear about horrible things that happen sometimes on the Internet. I did just that, and David faxed me through a copy of his birth certificate and copies of letters that I had written to the Adoption Society. I just couldn't believe it. He had found me, after all the years I had been trying, and he had found me, through FriendsReunited. I was walking around in a dream. The e-mails were flying thick and fast between us, and then he phoned me. That was fantastic.

To hear his voice for the first time: WOW! I was petrified. I didn't know what his reaction was going to be, whether he was going to blame me for what had happened. I shouldn't have worried. He fully understands why I had to give him up and doesn't blame me at all. Even his mum, Andrea, who adopted him, phoned me and she was so lovely. It was so easy to talk to her, as though I had known her for years.

Well, on 12 December 2001, I met David for the first time. I was so scared at that first meeting. David, my husband, Reg, and I went to the pub first and then David came down home and stayed chatting for about three hours. I must admit, my stomach was turning somersaults all the time. I just kept looking at him thinking, 'He's my son'. That Christmas I had my first Christmas card from him and was able to send my first card to him. That was great. His mum, Andrea, also sent me a Christmas card with a photo album with pictures of David as he was growing up. To me, that was the most beautiful thing anyone had ever done for me, just knowing that she was in full agreement with us meeting up was great. There aren't many adoptive parents that would be so understanding. I cannot thank her enough for that. Then, eventually, in July last year, David met my brother, Ian, for the first time. They got on terrifically and Ian thinks he is absolutely fantastic. He's chuffed to bits to have at last met his nephew.

I think I am the luckiest person alive, and my life is now complete.

Every year, on 1 March, I used to think of David and wonder what he was doing and what he was like, now I know!

Dot Warman, Plumstead

Nine Months

A year ago, I found my birth mother using the name search on FriendsReunited. I was adopted before 1972 and the break was supposed to be forever with no comeback for either side. So last July [2002] I put my natural mother's name in and all her details popped up ... she was the only one and it was definitely her!

So, I bucked up the courage to e-mail her: 'If this is inappropriate, then I apologise, but what does 12 January 1968 mean to you?'

The reply came back: 'Jeremy I have been looking for you for years. My husband and other three children know about you and we would all love contact!'

We corresponded by e-mail for the next month or so before meeting last August. My mother explained so much to me! She also explained that she had spent the last 15 years leaving messages for me on teletext, missing person sites etc, and had all but given up finding me.

The twist in this story is that two weeks after I found my mother she was diagnosed with secondary cancer of the liver and sadly she died some weeks ago – I was with her when she died. So thank you to FriendsReunited for giving me nine wonderful months with my late mother.

Jeremy Swan

Thirty Two Years Of Hurt

FriendsReunited changed my life and made a dream come true. In 1970 whilst still at school I became pregnant and had a baby boy. I was forced to hand him over for adoption by my grandparents who told me I was not allowed to keep him. I nursed him for ten days in hospital, then he was taken from me and given to his adoptive parents.

I spent years grieving for my son. I ran away from home and had lots of problems. I just wanted to get rid of the pain of losing my baby.

I spent the next 32 years burying the pain, but always loving my son and wanting to know where he was. I always told my other children about him, he was never kept a dark secret. Then in 2001 a friend told me about the website. I never imagined it would change my life. I joined in August and made contact with primary school friends that I had not heard from for over 30 years. It was amazing to talk to old friends.

Then in January 2002, I received an e-mail from my son Martin. He had put my name into your search engine, and after 13 years of searching finally found me. We have had very emotional meetings, getting to know each other, and it has been wonderful for us to finally meet. I have also met my granddaughter!

Yvonne

It's become a cliché now: kids say the most embarrassing things. But, like all the best clichés ('It's what he would've wanted ... Things ain't what they used to be ... It was a game of two halves'), there's more than a grain of universal truth in it. Here are a few youngsters that deserve a clip round the ear.

'I caused my parents endless embarrassment; like the time we were staying at the Tregenna Castle Hotel and, after supper, my parents told me it was time to go to bed and I recited the little rhyme:

Night, night, sleep tight
And don't let the bed-bugs bite,
If they do, take your shoe
And knock them black and blue!

All the other patrons within earshot looked quite horrified.'

'We were staying with my in-laws for the weekend, along with our small chidren. Little Kyle was still being potty-trained and so either I, or his granpa, would accompany him to the toilet. At the big family supper, with all the aunts and uncles present, he announced, "Daddy, Grampa's p***s is bigger than yours!"'

'I went to the doctor to have my third pregnancy confirmed, taking with me my four-year old, Laura. She (allegedly) sat by the desk whilst I went behind the screen to be examined. On a packed bus going home, quite a distance from the surgery, she shouts out loudly, "Mummy, why did you take your knickers off for that man?" All eyes were upon me and I just wanted to curl up and die.'

'My eldest, who was four at the time, proceeded to tell everyone in the hairdresser's that I had a "fluffy foof" and her daddy had a "yukky todger"! Call your bits what you like, but everybody got the gist of it. I wanted to die! If that wasn't bad enough, she said the same thing at the in-laws. Luckily they are both a bit "mutton jeff".'

'When my daughter was four we went to my in-laws for Sunday dinner. During dinner, my sweet, adorable child proceeds to say, "Grandma, do you know my mum and dad have sex?" I thought my mother-in-law was going to keel over right there and then. My father-in-law was laughing so hard the tears were running down his face. My hubby and I were mortified. On the way home I asked my daughter how she knew about sex, and she shrugged and said, "I don't know." I asked her what she thought it meant and she replied, "It's kissing and cuddling." Phew, what a relief, my little angel was still just that.'

'While in the hardware store with my two small children, one of the clerks asked me if the little boy was mine. My son had just become potty-trained and proudly showed me the huge "number-two" he had done in one of the toilets on display in the bathroom fixtures section!'

'Standing in the post office queue one day with my six-year old daughter and my 18-month-old son, just after we had taken him for his innoculations, my daughter shouted at the top of her voice, "Daddy, did you have to have erections when you were a boy?" I had a very hard job explaining to everyone that she meant injections!'

'My ten-year-old boy and I often practise wrestling moves on each other. One day, whilst we were out shopping and behaving like a couple of kids, I attempted a "full nelson" at the checkout in Iceland. Instead of playing along, he yelled at the top of his voice: "Help, my dad's molesting me!" I went bright red, and my wife smacked me!'

'My wife was in a queue at a checkout once where another mother was struggling with an unruly girl. The girl shouted at the top of her voice, "If you don't let me have some sweets, I'll tell Nana that I saw you kissing daddy's *****!" Well you can guess the rest. Mother and child left the shopping and departed post haste.'

Altogether Now

The brilliant premise of the John Cusack comedy *Grosse Point Blank* is that of a ten-year high school reunion in a Detroit suburb where one ex-pupil turns up and has to hide the fact that he is now a hired assassin. School reunions are rarely that dramatic – and FriendsReunited has yet to register its first hitman – but they're becoming ever more popular in the UK. Though not as pathologically nostalgic as the Brits, the Americans started the craze, but then over there school ends with a prom and graduation yearbook; here it just kind of fizzles out. Not everybody likes the idea of an organised reunion – indeed, one less than happy story here concerns a clash of organisers – but when it all comes together, such an occasion can not only provide laughs, it can also, as one member has it, 'lay ghosts to rest'. The best reunions are invariably those that form organically around a small group, but the banners-and-punch kind can go off with a bang too. It's amazing how often confronting the school bully over a plate of spinach parcels comes up too. Chances are, he turned out to be a pussycat. And not a contract killer.

Giving A Tucker An Even Break

There was a guy I hated at school, Andrew Tucker – he lived up the road from me as a child. He was one of those really annoying, mickey-taking boys who always managed to get everyone on his side.

As a child I was very plump, all through infants, juniors and senior school I had to put up with his immature antics of pretending to pop me with his imaginary pin. I hated him, he made my life hell. Anyway, at the age of 14, his parents decided to emigrate to Australia. What a relief! I was finally free of him. The strange thing was that I kind of missed him and as I grew into a young lady the weight was shed and I became our local Carnival queen. How I wished Andrew Tucker could have seen me. (Maybe his taunts helped me!)

Time sailed by, I married and had three beautiful daughters. As the children started school and using computers, I decided to get a second-hand computer. Whilst trying out different websites I came across FriendsReunited. What a website!

Being a mum and holding down my part-time job, I had lost contact with many of my friends, so seeing all these old names got me thinking about school. One name stared back at me from the many names from my school year... Andrew Tucker!

This was payback time. I made this my first priority. I e-mailed him telling him how he had made my early school years hell, and told him I wanted an apology after 22 years. I didn't have to wait long, he e-mailed me from Australia telling me how he was so very sorry and how he wanted to make it up to me.

We kept in regular contact through the computer. He told me how he had two children of his own and how he missed England. He spoke to my husband through e-mails and my children too, and became a part of our lives in a way.

After many e-mails, he told me how much he wanted to come home. I suggested a school reunion. He told me this was an excellent idea. So straight away I got e-mailing and arranging a reunion. The e-mails came flooding in! The ball was rolling and a date was set for Friday, 9 May 2003. Andrew didn't let me down, he booked his ticket and told me he was going to make it to the reunion, only he didn't tell me it was to stay in England for good!

I received a phone call this Sunday just gone to say that he was at our local train station. I couldn't believe it. I went and picked him up with my family. And guess what? He is the nicest, sweetest, most interesting guy I know. He is staying in London now. He's made such a commitment. He's coming to the reunion on Friday and I can't wait to see him again. My family love him.

It just goes to show you that people do change. From being my enemy, he is now one of my best friends.

Suzanne Goodwin, Shoeburyness, Essex

Waiting For Kenneth

I attended the Meadway Comprehensive School in Tilehurst, Reading from 1982–89, and have kept in contact with my best friends over the years. But I have always wondered what had happened to a few others.

When I heard about the FriendsReunited website a few years back, I joined up, delighted to get back in touch with people. Eventually, a reunion was suggested, and I put together plans to hold an event in the main hall of the sports centre next to (and part of) the school.

I placed items in local papers but the main method of spreading the news, however, was undoubtedly through the FriendsReunited website. I e-mailed hundreds of people over the next few weeks as far back as the class of 1976 and as far forward (from my year) as 1996. I also contacted the school and managed to contact a great many of the teachers who had taught us over the years.

By the day of the event, we had sold about 100 tickets and were slightly worried that we would make a loss. Thankfully about 50 people turned up on the door.

I was pleased to see everyone that attended and recognised nearly everyone who'd been at the school when I had – that's a spread of 13 years! Some people were only barely recognisable (older, bigger, balder etc), whilst others hadn't changed at all – even the style of clothes – a couple of people I hadn't seen for ten years looked exactly how I remembered them! There was a good-humoured drunken discussion between a former 'disruptive type' and one of the music teachers. The music teacher told him what a pain he'd been at the school and, although still clearly a bit of a joker, he apologised and they had a good laugh about it.

A lad from my year, who'd had a crush on one girl, met her again and carried on wooing her in a drunken state. He didn't get anywhere ...

One of the ladies from the class of '76 got extremely drunk and was sick around the back of the sports hall! She later told me she didn't remember leaving the event but did remember that she had had a good time. She was so enthused by the event, and by meeting people again from all those years ago, that she organised her own reunion just for her year.

One drunken bloke, whom I'd hardly spoken to whilst at school, kept telling me what a great bloke I was for organising everything and trying to hug me! I think he meant well!

The ex-pupils included Simone Jacobs, the former 100m and 200m Olympic sprinter, and BBC local newsreader Allen Sinclair. Sadly, former pupil (class of '77) Kenneth Brannagh did not attend.

An eighties-style school disco towards the end of the evening was well received and seemed the perfect end to a great evening. I am starting to think about the next big reunion for the whole school and will be looking to use the FriendsReunited website again to contact everyone.

Oliver Hunter, Northampton

Here's To You, Mrs Robinson

I migrated as a 'Ten Pound Pom' from Pendleton, Lancashire to Perth, in Western Australia. After eight years, I became a widow without anyone to lean on.

Then I realised home is were the heart is: the UK. It took many years to save for a return trip. I placed my notice in the *Manchester Evening News* in 1993.

One hundred and twenty-five cousins and classmates etc arrived at my reunion! Many I recognised after all the years. Photographs were taken, addresses exchanged; I took my old photo albums and we laughed over tales of Wellington Street and Enys Street schools, wearing Siren Suits to keep out the cold. Mrs Robinson was one of my favourite teachers.

Through the Internet, I tried tracing my old teachers. I was reunited with Mrs Robinson, we now talk regularly on the phone. I thought she would be at least 95 now – but lo and behold she is in her late 70s! I am 66 now. To a child, a married lady was old, hence my rude awakening when I realised there was only 11 years' difference.

Then came FriendsReunited. My whole world came alive, friends from everywhere turn up on my PC. Through FriendsReunited, over the last two years, I have been able to put many of her pupils in touch with her again.

Mrs Robinson recently said to me, 'Rita, you live soooo far away and yet people who live so near never realised I was still alive till you told them!' She also told me of her dismay when she was originally told she would be assigned to Wellington St School and its 'urchins'. All these years later, she confessed how proud she was of her pupils now. 'Ninety per cent grew up with nothing and became something.' A credit to us, was how she put it!

I am proud to say I was one of those 'urchins'. I still have a pair of clogs here in my home!

I feel I have come 'home', even though I still live in Western Australia. Thank God for FriendsReunited. I did go to the UK again in 1998 but FriendsReunited is cheaper, ha ha!

Rita Cowan (née Hewitson), Perth, Western Australia

This Used To Be My Playground

I arranged a reunion for my infant/junior school, Copenhagen Primary School. I held it in the school, which I had not been back to since the early sixties. I was expecting about 30 people, and 65 arrived, including a lady in her eighties.

The school caretaker was a diamond, he let us have the run of the school. Looking in classrooms brought back so many memories for us all. The biggest thrill at seeing the school was the playground, which was on the roof. We all said that nothing had changed. I met people who lived in the street where I lived, a cousin, girls I had started nursery with, and lots of people I didn't know, but we all had so much in common. We had all lived in London in the forties, fifties and sixties and that's all that mattered. Nobody asked what we were doing now. There could have been millionaires or tramps there, it didn't matter, we had just all gone to the same school and had wonderful memories of real people.

We are going to do it all again next year, only this time I think more people will be there.

Lynda Worth (née Pace), London

Reunion Blues

I had fantastic memories of attending an all-girls school in Plymouth, which had close links with the local all-boys school. I boarded at the school for five years and was very much part of the family and part of the cool gang.

When I left in 1988 to go to college, I was devastated to be leaving my friends as we all went our separate ways. We kept in touch for a while, but as the years went by we lost contact, until this website appeared.

Absolutely delighted, I made contact with old friends I hadn't heard from in years. I was living in California at the time, so I began to arrange a reunion with one of my old best friends.

I had been working as a wedding co-ordinator for some time and so, naturally, was incredibly excited about being part of the arrangements for such an event. I had believed I was working to the same idea as my friend, when totally out of the blue, she decided she didn't want to have such a large event after all and wanted a smaller one in a pub which would supposedly be more intimate.

She took it upon herself to send an incredibly biased e-mail to people, which unfortunately made my ideas look pathetic and over the top.

Various e-mails were sent back and forth until, despite all the research I had put into the event, I felt so upset and a complete stranger to her and my old friends, that I pulled out of the reunion altogether.

I have heard that a very small reunion did take place and I know some of the girls are still in touch with each other, but I feel so upset about it all that I honestly wish the past had been left in the past.

The bad memories of school life had faded over the years in favour of the good times and it is only since getting in touch with people and especially this one girl in particular, that you remember that things weren't so great after all.

Tracey Duke, Devon

You May Say I'm A Dreamer

I managed to get in touch with a friend called Pat Hoefling through FriendsReunited, with whom I had gone through primary school and into senior school. Apparently, at primary school, the teacher used to call us 'Dream 1' and 'Dream 2', for obvious reasons – we weren't listening, we were in our own little world.

I also managed to contact girls from my primary school (bearing in mind this was approximately 57 years ago), and we had a reunion at a local restaurant recently. I learned from one of them that together we had managed to smash my mother's cherished dinner service. How, I don't know!

Beryl Baird, Hemel Hempstead

Gobsmacked!

In January 2002, during a telephone conversation with an old school friend Fiona, she mentioned that someone had told her about the FriendsReunited website. As she didn't have a PC, she asked me to investigate and see if there was anyone registered on there that we knew. So I found the website and registered with my senior school – Merrywood Girls, in Bristol.

I found virtually all of my old crowd listed under 1984–85! I sat there completely gobsmacked reading how my many friends' lives had been over the past 17 years – they all still lived locally. How had we managed not to bump into each other when we all lived so close?

The first seven days were a barrage of e-mails to and from each other, basically covering our life histories so far. It was fascinating and exciting at the same time. We were all in agreement that we had to meet up and the sooner the better. So we set a date, time and venue and arranged our first reunion.

I was in such a state leading up to the day, that I had to book the day off work and the day off afterwards, as I couldn't control my nervousness and excitement. I had previously been through a bad bout of depression and had been on medication for 18 months. My life was completely solitary and I had not had a social life for over three years. As you can imagine, the reunion was a big event for me and would be a judge of my recovery so far.

The evening arrived and I pulled up in the pub car park. I was physically shaking and had to stand outside the pub taking deep breaths. It was like going on a blind date – or worse! I prayed that I was not the first to arrive and that I wouldn't make a fool of myself by not recognising anyone! I braced myself, walked into the pub and found five of my old friends sitting at a table. Everyone was laughing and joking and I sat down, cracked a couple of 'old days' comments and within five minutes, it was like the past 17 years had never happened.

The night flew by and before we knew it, the pub had closed and there we all were sat in a closed pub. The landlord realised it was a reunion and didn't like to interrupt us!

Since then, we all speak or e-mail every week. We meet every 6–8 weeks for meals, nights outs etc, and have recently started to introduce our partners/husbands and children to each other. Surprisingly, the husbands all get along well and have virtually the same hobbies and interests.

I have since registered on my old junior school and work sites, and I can't believe how my life has changed these past 18 months. By having the courage to contact my old friends, it gave me the confidence to change other things in my life as well.

I now have a wonderful fiancé and we have bought a fantastic house together. Life just gets better and better...

Joanna Watkins, Bristol

Bully For You

This is not an overly exciting story, but may affect a lot of people. I was not part of the in-crowd at school. I wasn't cool, but I wasn't a nerd. The girls made my life hell with emotional-style bullying and, consequently, I have lived the rest of my life terribly lacking in confidence. I joined FriendsReunited and learnt last year of a reunion. I had actually started trying to organise a reunion, but had had to give up due to personal problems.

Despite living in northern Scotland and having a journey of 12 hours to make it, I decided to go.

Heart in my mouth and husband in tow, I made it through the door without having a panic attack. Oh my God! The girls who made my life hell were both there and one of them didn't recognise me, as neither did ninety per cent of my classmates who were there. I was flattered and complimented and my husband said the thing he enjoyed most was the glow around me and the look on my face.

I am so glad I went. I've laid quite a few personal ghosts to rest. I would have to recommend to anyone who has doubts about attending a reunion to pluck up their courage and go, even if you need to take a friend with you for support. That journey was the best thing that I've done in many years. Go for it – good luck.

Tina Rae, Inverness, Moray

One, Two, Three

Reunion 1. Just recently I returned to England from Australia to celebrate the centenary anniversary of the teachers college I attended in the early 70s, Bedford Physical Education College. About 15 from our year, 1972, attended and about 200 in total, with the oldest lady having left the college in 1939. We all had a fabulous weekend and took some great photos, especially the one of us doing gymnastics at 2 o'clock in the morning! (Well we were all phys ed teachers once.) We were allowed to stay in the old college dorms. It was a wonderful time and brought back many memories.

Reunion 2. A week later I met up with and went walking in the Dales with four other friends who had been at Saint Monica's Convent, Skipton with me in 1965. We walked and talked and then we visited our old convent where we had been boarders. What memories that brought back. In the evening we met up with six more friends who had been at school in our year and we had a wonderful night in Gassington, reminiscing about the old times. Some of us are meeting up again in Australia in five years' time, for a walking and talking holiday.

Reunion 3. The third weekend five of us from St Joseph's College in Bradford (class of '69) met in Birmingham and had a wonderful day catching up on news from past and present about ourselves and other friends from the past.

None of these reunions would have happened if it hadn't been for FriendsReunited.

Coppelia Tingley (née Hetherinton), Perth, Western Australia

Where Are They Now?

I attended an annual school reunion for the first time this year for Pontypridd Boys Grammar School, which effectively ceased to be in 1975.

I found out about the annual reunion of old boys from a friend I found on FriendsReunited. So we decided to contact the 'Hon Sec', who was our old (well he is now) chemistry teacher.

We went to the 'bash' and, very oddly, we were in some sort of time warp! We were the only three 'lads' of our age (46 years young) from a possible 100 or so ex-pupils of our year... and the next oldest 'old boy' had to be 65 years old! Where, I wonder, were the 2000 'old boys' between our age and the mid-sixties?

I know a lot have moved away, many out of the country, but still...

We'll go again next year but how many will have passed on, some there were over 80!?

And how many old boys will there be attending when we reach retirement age? Perhaps only we three? Sad but somewhat 'Twilight Zone'...

Huw D Jones, Pontypridd, Mid Glamorgan

The Brinsley Schwarz Connection

Jaki and I went to Berrymede Infants School in Acton, London. We first met in 1954 when we both started in the kindergarten class. She was two months older than me and also taller. I was a little elfin type with short hair, a cheeky face and dimples. She had long hair scraped back into a ponytail. I remember thinking that I wanted to be like her.

We made friends immediately and were inseparable for the next two years until she moved to Hale in Cornwall with her parents. I was devastated and missed her terribly. I often thought about her because we had quite a close relationship. We were too young to write letters to each other and my parents thought that it was a good thing for us to be separated, because I relied on Jaki so much. I made lots of new friends and life moved on.

My mum still lives in the house that I was born in and when my husband and I went to visit her we often passed the house where Jaki used to live. I'd always say to him, 'That's where my friend used to live,' and he would patiently answer, 'Oh is it?' as if it was the first time I'd mentioned it. I never forgot her.

I joined FriendsReunited a long time ago and have corresponded with lots of my old friends from primary and secondary school and also from my old college too. Then out of the blue I received an e-mail from my old friend Jaki. I just could not believe it. I wrote back immediately recounting everything that I could remember of the two years we were friends. She was astounded how I could remember minute details about her house and garden.

The story could end here but there is more, for you see our lives went on to be very similar — so similar that our paths have crossed on more than one occasion and we didn't realise.

I married Ian Gomm who was a member of the cult country rock group Brinsley Schwarz back in the early seventies. One of their roadies went on to play bass guitar in Hawkwind. Jaki used to be the girlfriend of one of the drummers in Hawkwind. We both went to the first Glastonbury festival and sat on stage behind the bands.

We both love music: she plays drums and I play saxophone. We both dance and sing and work in schools with young people. We both called one of our sons Sam.

The most incredible part of this story is that Jaki was outside my house in Llanfair Caereinion, Powys the Easter before she had contacted me, when she was recording with her group Space Ritual at the studio in mid-Wales where my husband used to work. She said to her companions that she really liked my house and wondered who lived there. My husband Ian happened to be looking out of the window at the time and saw the group and remarked to me that there were people outside that looked like they were going to record at the studio. I didn't even go to look!

We eventually met on 18 July 2003, in a campsite beside Bala Lake in the picturesque hills of North Wales where she was accompanying a group of young people who were taking part in the Duke of Edinburgh Award Scheme. I recognised her straight away and she said that I hadn't changed either except for my long hair and weight gain. I still have the dimples and the cheeky face. She was wearing a pair of fairy earrings exactly the same as mine.

We spoke together for about six hours non-stop! We have so many common interests although we have lived completely different kinds of lives. I find it quite incredible how at such a young age we recognised something in each other that we liked and a bond was made. Obviously we hadn't reached our full potential at that time but we both knew that we were happy when we were together. I can't remember ever falling out with her either.

We would never have found each other again if it weren't for FriendsReunited. Jaki is thinking about moving to Wales and I am looking out for a house for her nearby. I can't wait for us to play music together and maybe even form a band of old ladies; after all 53 isn't that old is it? Watch this space!

Karen Ingold, Powys

Golden Grahame

I met up with an old pal from school for a beer last year, as we both live in Harrow, having moved from Middlesbrough many years before.

We talked about all the teachers, the girls we fancied, drank more beer and generally had a great evening remembering the school and drinking.

After a few hours, the beer taking its toll, it was time to leave. I said, 'Hey, Grahame, next time we meet up I'll bring the photos of the chess team.'

'Why?' said Grahame. 'I wasn't in the chess team!'

I'd spent three hours having a good, old chinwag and getting pissed with *completely* the *wrong* Grahame Chapman.

Chris Patterson, Harrow, Middlesex

Nothing divides opinion like pop music. After all, one man's 'Meat Is Murder' is another man's 'Poison Arrow'. Whether the message boarders are arguing the merits of S Club 7 or 'O Superman' or dissecting Wombles lyrics, there is always discord along with harmony.

Most hated records?

'The record I hate most is "Lovely Day" by Bill Withers.'

'Setting aside all the novelty rubbish, the worst record I've ever heard is "MacArthur Park" by Richard Harris.'

'Can anyone remember (not that you'd want to) Tony Blackburn's *frightful* record in the seventies called "Chop Chop Chop"? Almost as ghastly is "Black is Black", but thankfully I don't remember who visited this monstrosity upon us. I just recall he gets in the coffin with her in the end. Should have stayed there.'

'Renée & Renato — "Save Your Love" (exactly *who* bought this?) and Billy Ray Cyrus' "Achy Breaky Heart" — I break out in hives when I hear this.'

'Anything that ends in "by Celine Dion" and I especially hate "I Will Always Love You" by Whitney Houston. If anyone tries to play that one at my funeral, I will always *haunt* them.'

'Joe Dolce — "Shaddap You Face" — crap.'

'My worst song ever has to be "Love Shack" by the B-52s — bloody annoying.'

'I hate "Bohemian Rhapsody" with a vengeance.'

'I *hate hate hate* ... I don't even want to write it... here goes: "O Superman" — Loni Anderson. I don't even care if that's not her correct name!' [Actually, the poor woman's name is 'Laurie' — Ed]

Stupid lyrics

'Yesterday I heard "I'm Still Waiting" by Diana Ross on the radio and it struck me that the line "He could see I had no eyes" is a daft line. What are your favourite stupid lyrics?'

'What about "Remember You're A Womble". How on earth could you forget that you were a Womble?'

'Your trouser cuffs are dirty
And your shoes are laced up wrong
You'd better take off your homburg
Cos your overcoat is too long.

"Homburg" by Procul Harum.'

Which music would you like to hear in restaurants?

'Coldplay – all the time! They've got everything in their album to get you really enjoying your meal. Or am I just a fanatic?'

'I've been to a little Indian restaurant where the ornaments are from Spain and Greece and the music is usually Engelbert Humperdinck, but the food is great and it's so quirky but it works.'

'Well I think that Janis Ian and Boz Scaggs go with most food. However Sean Keane is more of a specialist taste maybe for that very special evening.'

'I know a little Italian place that likes to put on the local radio station at full blast, but doesn't tune its radio in properly. I wonder why I don't go there any more... I also asked for French dressing for a salad once and they had to nip to the corner shop to get it.'

Favourite Songs from 1970s Advertisements

'I liked the Coke ad's "I'd Like To Teach the World to Sing".'

'Cresta bear, how could I forget about that one: "I don't wanna drink the ocean, cause man that's really rough/But when it comes to Cresta here's one bear that just can't get enough" – well something like that.

'"Do the shake and vac and put the freshness back..." Oh dear, pitiful!'

Best S Club 7 Song

'I believe the best S Club 7 song was "Bring It All Back". What do the rest of you think?'

'I think that the best S Club 7 song was "Don't Stop Movin'". It was a great party anthem.'

'Thinking about some of the songs S Club did. Do you know I can't think of any of them except "Say Goodbye", or was that Steps...?'

'Best S Club song??? It's a bit like asking me what's the best way to be castrated, *there isn't one*!!'

'I like most of their songs, but "Reach" is my fave.'

Best Beard in Rock

'Who has the best beard in Rock? ZZ Top, bass player from Queens Of The Stone Age, Craig David??'

'Jimmy Page... circa 1970.'

'From a purely historical point of view – Mr Phillip Collins circa 1979 A ginger/blond shock – nasty.'

'Jim Morrison – considering his youth, he managed to look pretty grizzly.'

The Beatles

'Am I the only one who hates the mop tops?'

'Was it true Ringo took a suitcase full of baked beans to India when they met the Maharishi, just so he didn't have to eat the food?'

'Mate, it's only music, and I'm afraid that if everybody likes them... well everybody likes them. Don't worry about it.'

War And Peace

Don't mention the war. In fact, do. The Second World War was the defining
event of the twentieth century, and for those who can remember it, the
defining event of their lives. Anyone born since 1945, who knows war only as
TV news footage shot in deserts and jungles far away, may find it difficult to
truly grasp the notion that the Blitz united people; that the fear of invasion
and death made them stronger, more resilient. Evacuation from town to
country — impossible for today's youngsters to imagine — helped forge
fleeting friendships, many of which have been rekindled with the help of
FriendsReunited. Air raid shelters and whistling doodlebugs also feature
prominently in the collective memory, as do windows criss-crossed with
brown tape and the rare treat that was a banana. It seems glib to speak, as
newspapers do, of having 'a good war' or 'a bad war', but if there's one thing
that comes out of these stories, it's that for all the fear and destruction, the
war also brought people closer together. It certainly wasn't 'a phoney war'.
Altogether now: 'There'll be bluebirds over...'

Some Foreign Field

While researching my family history I came across a copy of a family tree going back many generations. I had a great-uncle, Edward Britton, on my father's side who had been killed in action in Ypres in 1917 aged 27. He has no grave, just an inscription on the Menin Gate in Belgium. I kept thinking about this brave soldier and often wondered what he had looked like. I possessed no photographs.

Another name on the family tree was a girl called Karen Britton. Like myself she would have been the great-niece of this soldier. I entered her name and a number of Karen Brittons came up. By elimination I was able to find one who lived in Kent and left school in the right approximate year. I e-mailed her and the next day she replied: I had found the right Karen Britton, possibly my third cousin.

I told her I was researching my family tree and did her father have any old photographs? To cut a long story short, I am now in possession of several photogaphs of not only my own grandfather as a child (who I never knew) but photographs of the soldier Edward in uniform and many more photographs of great-uncles, great-aunts and great-great grandmother. Had it not been for FriendsReunited I would never have traced my cousin and would never have seen any of these priceless photographs. I am thrilled.

Suzanne Whinnett

The Smell Of Gran

I was born in Miles Platting, Manchester, in 1931. Every Sunday afternoon my mam used to take me to see my gran, while Dad was 'sleeping it off'. The pub used to close at two on a Sunday so he'd come home very cheerful

and let me have a bit of his dinner that Mam had kept warm over a pan of
hot water. We always had ours at half past twelve, a civilised time, she said.

We went to Gran's by tram, but we had a long way to walk from the tram
stop at the other end. Mam used to walk very fast and I had to run to keep up
with her. She was always mad at something and that made her shout at me a
lot. She made me wear my Sunday coat with covered buttons and a matching
hat just like Princess Margaret and Princess Elizabeth used to wear. But
mine had to last a long time and some of the time it was too long and then it
was too short. Mam said it didn't matter if my frock dangled down.

Most of all, I remember the smell of Gran. Like all the old women where
she lived, she wore clogs that you could see your face in, a fringed black
shawl and a big apron. She was very fat and when she laughed every bit of
her shook up and down. I used to try and get my arms round her middle
and she'd stroke my hair, or rub my back while she whistled 'Lily of
Laguna' to me. That's when I got the smell, and if I try hard, I can
remember it, a musty, sweetish smell – not dirty, but warm and lasting.
Gran used to spoil Mam. Nearly every Sunday there was a lovely smell in
the kitchen. She cooked in a little oven at the side of the fireplace. A
special treat was a cheese-and-onion pie baked in a saucer. No one else
could have any. As soon as it was cool enough, Gran used to watch Mam
eating it, stretching the hot cheese on her fork and spilling little bits of
onion on the scrubbed table. They didn't talk much, but they looked happy
about something. There was usually a bit of pastry left over to make me a
couple of jam tarts.

Gran was a real worry when the air raids started. She wouldn't go to the
shelter. Once there was a big explosion near her house and she was blown
out of bed. She was furious and told us that she picked herself up and
climbed back into bed. She always said that if it were her time to go, she'd go
whether she was in the shelter or not.

One Sunday, one of Gran's neighbours stopped us in the street. He told us
that German machine gunners had come screaming down the street that
week. (Gran lived near a big munitions factory.) Everyone threw themselves
on the ground as the planes swooped. He even showed us the holes in the
walls. But he said that Gran had just stood there shaking her fist at the sky
shouting, 'You won't frighten me Mr Schickelgruber!' Mam told her she was

lucky to be alive and she should have done what everyone else did. Gran said she'd only just put a clean apron on, and it had been raining.

I don't remember when she died. I know it was Mam who found her where she'd fallen in front of the fireplace. She'd burned her hand and broken the iron hob trying to get up. They said it was dropsy, but Mam said what's the use of asking questions, you just have to get on with it.

We had a very little funeral on a cold, wet day. Dad took the day off work and held my hand all the time. Then we went to tea at a café, but Mam didn't want anything to eat. I bet she'd have loved a cheese and onion pie on a saucer.

© **Doreen Pascal-Murray (née Taylor), Melbourne, Australia**

Tremors

The school I went to, Acland Burghley School in North London, was rebuilt next to an old 'bomb site'. Years after leaving school I was watching a television programme about a bomb being found and it being dismantled, the site of this bomb being right next to my old school. This was especially surprising and a little scary, as trains used to run under the school, and when we used to sit in the gym that was nearest to the bomb site, you could feel the tremor as the trains went under it.

Jenny Hart, Watford, Herts

Louder Than Bombs

My name is Dennis; my friend's name is Roy. This is the story of how FriendsReunited was instrumental in putting us in touch with each other after losing contact for nearly 60 years.

The story starts in 1943, the latter part of World War Two, when I lived in Norton-on-Tees, a small village on the north-east coast near Middlesbrough. I was eight years old at the time. I am now almost 68.

This was a time when the Germans were bombing London day and night in a last-ditch effort to burn London and bring Britain to its knees. The Germans were starting to use unmanned flying bombs, known as V1s and, later, V2s, which were causing havoc in and around London. Living in London was a nightmare and the authorities were encouraging parents to send their children to the country under a government-organised evacuation scheme.

My friend Roy lived in London, he had been evacuated previously, but when the bombing eased, he returned home. Soon after his return, the Blitz started and it was a good time for him to be evacuated again. This proved to be the start of our short but lasting friendship. This extract from one of his e-mails describes his feelings:

'You asked how I felt as a nine-year-old arriving in Norton. Well, by then I was a hardened evacuee type. I was first evacuated with the general exodus from London in 1939 and sent alone to St Just in Cornwall at the age of four or five. I well remember that, but I do not recall being particularly traumatised. Maybe, in a sense, it was the right age, too young to really appreciate the significance.

I always say that Hitler was after me personally because, all the time I was there, it was during what was known as the phoney war, so after a while in 1940/41, my mother decided to have me back home. Now, Adolf obviously got to know about this, so he let loose the first London Blitz, bombing me for something like 73 consecutive nights. Mum obviously regarded me as a bit of a Jonah, so she sent me away again and... the bombing stopped! So that's how I finished up in Norton about 1943.

I returned to London just in time for the bombardment from flying bombs followed by V2 rockets, but despite all that effort he missed me and had to give up!'

I remember news spreading in the village that some evacuees were coming. Anyone with a spare room and without a very good reason for not offering accommodation was told they were to get a 'billet'.

I had an aunt and uncle who were relatively wealthy, lived in a large house with a big garden and had no children, so they were cast-iron candidates for a 'billet'. They chose a girl.

When word got out that there was a busload of evacuees in the area I went to find them … along with almost all the local children for miles around! I remember looking at several green double-decker buses with their cargoes of young, very weary humanity, each clutching a small suitcase and the ubiquitous gas mask in its brown cardboard case slung by a piece of string across the chest; none appeared to be much older than I was. Roy was one of these young people who had been uprooted and taken many miles from home without knowing where they were going, or who was going to look after them.

One day, I was asked if I would like to meet Uncle Harry's evacuee. I don't know what I expected, but it was in the back of my mind that it would be a girl! That was when I met Roy and our friendship started. Roy describes his recollections of the first few hours at his new 'home' in the following extract:

'Harry fed me bananas and home-made ice cream and took me in his massive Morris 25 to Seaton Carew. I thought I had arrived in paradise and it proved, subsequently, to be almost that.'

Roy and I spent a lot of time together. We went on long walks in the countryside and fishing in the local streams with fishing rods that Uncle Harry had made for each of us. We also made many trips to the Cleveland hills, in an old-fashioned trap pulled by Mick the horse and driven by 'Matty' Parkin, one of Uncle Harry's employees. There were not many cars on the roads in those days, petrol was rationed and private motoring for pleasure was banned. There had to be a very good reason for a car to qualify for petrol coupons. Uncle Harry's pony and trap was a convenient way to get out into the country, where public transport was scarce, and a real adventure for children of our age. I asked him in one of my e-mails what he remembered about the pony and trap rides:

'It's one of my most cherished memories, collecting my mates and going on those wonderful trips into the Cleveland hills. No wonder I got a bit above myself. I would approach Uncle Harry at the office and ask, "Is Parkin doing anything in particular right now? If not, may I borrow him for a couple of hours?" Then, permission given, I would go down the yard and instruct Mr

Parkin to make the pony, Mick, ready for our adventure. I swear Mr Parkin addressed me as 'master' – what a little horror I must have been.'

After Roy returned to London, there was one brief holiday in London with my parents when we went to see him and we all went to London Zoo for the day. After that, contact was lost. Neither of us could have been interested in writing and were too young to appreciate the special friendship that we had developed.

It was fortunate that my family had kept some photographs from the period and I was able to find a professional portrait that must have been commissioned by Uncle Harry and given to my parents. I was also able to find a few very blurred Kodak Box Brownie photographs that featured the two of us, taken by another member of my family. It was a wonderful feeling when I found them.

As I got older, I started to ponder about my friend from London. I wrote to the last address I had and took to looking up his name in telephone directories wherever I went on business or holiday, but without success. In 1964 I accepted a job in Australia and we emigrated as a family.

When I found the FriendsReunited site, I registered and on 6 May 2002 I got the unexpected e-mail that put a smile on my face for days. Roy had been trying to find me too; he had put my name into the name search on the FriendsReunited site and there I was!

What I find surprising is the fact that we only knew each other for a short period, possibly only about 18 months and at such an early age it is easy to forget casual friendships. When you are on the other side of the world, it really means a lot to be reunited with your old friends.

Dennis G Dietz, Australia

My Ship Is Coming In

FriendsReunited enabled me to get in touch with an old shipmate Tony Dyer. We were both Engine Room Artificers who shared a cabin aboard HMS *Hectate*, a survey ship, from 1968 to 1970. I left the Royal Navy in 1970 and Tony went on to make a successful career as an Engineering Officer attaining the rank of Commander. I continued my career in various management positions within the engineering industry. Since making initial contact we have kept in touch by e-mail and we have met up twice and hope to continue in the coming years.

Graham Johnson

The Longest Day

I lived in Torquay, Devon, for the major part of the war and went to Croft Lodge School, Abbey Road. It was a convent school run by nuns of the order of Les Filles de la Croix and there was a boarding school attached to it called Stoodley Knowle, which was at Ilsham. On 6 June 1944, we went out of school at the usual time, but I found when I got to the bus station that no buses were running and no traffic was allowed along the seafront, which was my way home. The whole of the seafront between Torquay and Paignton had been closed off and I had to walk miles on a roundabout route to arrive home hours late.

I could see as I walked that the seafront was packed with every vehicle imaginable, lorries, jeeps, tanks, guns and soldiers, both American and British. It was like a great Armada. Next morning, they had gone and it was as if they had never been there. Then we heard the news D day had arrived.

Paula Sherlock, Bruton, Somerset

Lost Soles

In 1941 we were living in Red Lion Lane, in Woolwich, in London when I passed the scholarship exam, which could be taken by all ten-year-olds if their parents wished them to sit it. My mother was very pleased, especially as I was the second child in the family to have passed it.

But unfortunately there was a war on and there was little money around and I wondered if I, too, would be allowed to go to school in Abertillery with my sister. She would have attended Eltham Hill School, but because of the War, all the girls were now in Abertillery, Monmouthshire, which was an area considered to be safe to evacuate children to. (All the schools in London closed when the War started.)

Eventually, I made such a fuss about going to Abertillery, Mum gave in. She sorted all my sister's second-hand dresses, now too small for her, then we went to Eltham town because I was determined to have at least something new, if possible, so I got a blouse and a pair of shoes.

The day arrived when, together with my sister Irene, Mum saw us off on the train in London. On the train, my older sister said, 'It isn't nice here, so don't get excited.'

We arrived and made our own way to the house we were billeted in: 85 Tillery Street, Abertillery, with Mr and Mrs Williams. We each carried our scruffy cases. There was not much of a reception, in fact, hardly a 'hello' for me. Oh well, I thought, perhaps it might get better later.

Very soon, my sister suggested we walk up the garden out the back; we were both crying at being away from home and she thought this might cheer us up. I was wearing my one and only pair of new shoes.

There was a tall slag heap at the bottom of the garden, which looked exciting. It seemed massive. With excitement, I tried to climb up. I forgot where I was for a moment and when I came down my feet felt strange. I looked at the soles of my new shoes. The slag heap had cut large areas out of the soles. My sister and I were horrified – my only shoes! My sister gasped, I said, 'Don't worry, I won't tell anyone, I'll manage.'

I did manage right up until one day when my sister's form mistress, Miss Davies, said I could accompany her with her class, on a walk up the mountains. I set off, dressed in my sister's old shorts and my secretly destroyed shoes. Eventually, my pace was obviously becoming hindered by something or other and Miss Davies said, 'Mollie let me see your shoes?' She took one look at my feet and the woolly socks with the holes and the broken-up soles. I thought she was about to explode. I looked at my sister's face and she, too, was absolutely horrified. She looked as though she hoped I would disappear!

Miss Davies was carrying a rucksack. She rummaged in it for a while and produced a pair of high-heeled 'winkle-picker shoes' and she demanded that I wore these to protect my feet. It was absolutely ghastly trying to waddle along with those dreadful things, but I had to.

The next day, Miss Ozanne, our headmistress, heard about the trip up the mountain. There was more horror yet to come. She took me to the only shoe shop in Abertillery. It only sold men's and boys' shoes and I had to try a pair on. Oh yes, they did sort of fit, and how I hated the look of them, but I was more worried about the price though. Poor Mum – what would she think? Could she afford that sum? One thing, though – I had those shoes for ages – my brother looked quite good in them.

People soon realised that many [poor] children in London were roaming the streets, without school to attend, so things changed and London schools were asked to open again, if they could. The children would be safer in a school; although the War was still going on, it was terribly dangerous not to know where the children were.

Roan Emergency School For Girls was a school in London which was one of the first to reopen. My sister and I went there on the first day and they couldn't find enough chairs or books! It was better than nothing, though. We only stayed half a day and collected work to do at home!

Eltham Hill School followed shortly and we returned at last to where we should have started. It, too, had lots of security and wasn't working as it should, but eventually most girls returned from Abertillery and when the War actually ended it was super!

Mollie Peskett (née Bull), Broadstairs, Kent

'Her Other Evacuee'

I was reunited a few weeks ago with the school friend I was evacuated with in 1940 – after 55 years! We lost touch when my family moved to Cheshire just after the war. We were evacuated from Manchester to Colne in Lancashire. I have always kept in touch with the family we lived with. Although 'Grandma' passed away many years ago, her daughter 'Aunty', who is now 94, has wondered for many years what happened to her other evacuee. Thanks to FriendsReunited she will be able to see her before long.

Mrs Margaret Eccleston

Who Do You Think You Are Kidding?

I must admit I didn't like school very much, so in a way Hitler was almost my friend when lessons were interrupted. I can still remember happy hours singing 'Old MacDonald had a Farm', trying to out-do the noise of the bombs dropping, while in the school's underground shelters.

These shelters were always pitch black and full of fairly deep water. We had to crawl along the long seats attached to the wall. It must have been hell for the teachers. If you were at the far end of the shelter, you sometimes had a candle to play with.

One cold January morning in 1945, we were doing our lessons when an almighty 'bang' shook the school. We all dived under the desk as we were taught to do – then waited for the second explosion which always followed. V2 rockets had a ton of TNT in the warhead, but it was the rockets breaking the sound barrier that gave us warning. I remember parts of the ceiling falling down and my book covered in white dust. Most of the windows had disappeared, but luckily the criss-crossed brown sticky tape which was stuck on to them had saved the glass shattering into dangerous splinters. What I remember most was the water gushing out of the radiators. We all went out in the now-darkened corridors and, one by one, our teacher piggy-backed us through the water to retrieve our coats from the cloakroom. The strange thing is we hardly made a sound, which must have been quite a relief for the teachers.

I remember the joy in seeing a blackboard propped in the playground telling pupils 'No School Today'. Our school was too badly damaged after this V2 incident to re-open again. As far as I can remember, we didn't go back to that school for a year or two – that was until school officials caught up with us and sent me to another school (Salisbury Road Infants).

Peter Warren, Chelmsford, Essex

Goodbye Blackberry Way

The first indication that we had that war was imminent, was when we had to write in our school diaries that there was a 'crisis'. I thought that a very grown-up word and I'm not sure that we really knew what it meant.

I have always been an extrovert, and ready for adventure, so the War initially was just that, and I was not at all scared (until the bombs and land-mines started dropping on Liverpool and were getting too close for comfort).

Well, on 3 September 1939, we found ourselves on the platform at Lime Street Station, with our gas masks and luggage waiting to board the train. (I can still remember the rubbery smell of the mask.) Personally, I was so excited to be going to Aberystwyth for what seemed like a great long holiday. However, when I looked at my own dear mum, and others with tears in their eyes, I realised how hard it was for them to let us go. (No counselling for parents, or children, in those days.)

I remember that summer as being particularly hot, even for September, and we roamed around the castle ruins and were taken in the family car into the countryside and picked blackberries. Coming from the city we had not seen many blackberry bushes before.

We were untouched by the War, but even so, homesickness got the better of most of us and I was once more home by Christmas, in time for the bombing of Liverpool.

One thing that does stand out clearly in my memory is the early morning calling of the register. I think with hindsight how very tragic it must have seemed to our teacher. During the very heavy bombing regrettably sometimes children were killed. As the teacher called out each name waiting for a response, sometimes there was silence and someone would call out that she (that particular name) was killed last night. But we took it all in our stride; it was just part of our life in war-time. In my parents' house, I had a large attic room as my bedroom with the windows (closed of course) wide to the sky. I used to love to watch the searchlights criss-crossing in the sky, and then when I heard the ack-ack guns, I knew enemy planes were in the vicinity. Once, I actually saw a fight going on, caught in the searchlights, and was very annoyed when Mother repeatedly called me down to go in the shelter.

Joy Stone (née Barlow), Surrey

Give Me Shelter

I was at Middle Park School in Eltham, South London, during the War (not the First World War, I might add) and because of it we all had to have our classrooms on the ground floor (the school had three floors), since it was easier to get to the shelters that were across the large playground.

On this particular day in 1944 we were warned by our caretaker (who was on the roof of the school) that there was a doodlebug (a V1) heading our way. There was no air raid warning at that time for some reason and it was due to the caretaker that we all managed to get to the shelters.

We had only been down there a short while when we heard the V1 stop. We used to count to about 12 seconds and knew by then that it should have gone off. What we didn't know was that it was over the school!

When it went off, the explosion blew the iron door to our shelter in and on top of the middle row of forms that we were sitting on. It was a chance in a million that the teacher that usually sat on the end of that seat was away through illness (I had never known, in all the time I was at that school, her to miss a day). The escape hatch at the other end of the shelter blew up into the sky and a shower of flames and sparks came pouring into the shelter. We were all very scared for a while, but we all got out safely and no one was hurt.

People from the local shops and houses rushed over to see if we were all OK. The only person injured was the caretaker who was blown off of the school roof! I believe he had a broken leg — he was very lucky to have survived.

When we got home, our house and all those in the street were badly damaged, with no roofs or windows, slates all over the road and gardens, lamp posts and fences blown to pieces: our houses backed on to the school only about 500 yards away. The shops also suffered as a result of this. As food, of course, was on ration, there were not many, if any, luxuries to be found. But the local food shop had just had a delivery of red salmon, and it was all blown out into the road. I think the shopkeeper lost a few tins that day!!

Peter Anderson, Wingham, Kent

Greensleeves

I encouraged my dad Bert Day to register at his old schools in Liverpool. There were quite a few schools as his dad died when he was a baby and his mum and her three sons had to move around a lot as they were poor.

My dad was 81 in August this year and to be honest we didn't really think anyone would contact him. He seemed to be about the oldest person registered. Then he got an e-mail from the granddaughter of one of his army mates, Eric Read. They were at the D-Day landings in Normandy and they hadn't seen each other since the end of the war. My dad was delighted and flabbergasted to make contact with his old pal who now lives in Suffolk. He remembered that Eric's favourite tune was 'Greensleeves'.

Eric's granddaughter had written, 'Is that Bert Day from Liverpool who was at the Normandy landings? My granddad said he had a great sense of humour.' We sent an e-mail back with contact details and the information about Eric's favourite tune and soon after my dad was speaking on the telephone to his old pal.

Last year Eric and his wife came up to Liverpool for my dad's 80th birthday party in a Chinese restaurant and they had a great old time. I am so pleased that my dad met up with his old pal – the beaming smiles on the photographs sum it all up.

Jennie Day, Liverpool

Now that we have Trinny and Susannah, what not to wear has become something of a science. It wasn't always thus, and hair and fashion confessions from yesteryear never fail to entertain.

Hairstyles

'The "coupe savage" in the early eighties was bad. I had one by mistake once. It's where the hair is heavily layered and each layer was blown on to the face. Just your nose and mouth poked out. Foul.'

'OK, I admit I had the lot – Purdey, Lady Di, poodle perm, mullet, bob, bleached fringe and the rest dark.'

'I had a "Limahl from Kajagoogoo" when I was about nine, then grew my hair so that I could have the shaggy perm. It looked great with the dark blue eyeliner that we all used to pass round the toilets at break time! I'm surprised there weren't more eye infections in our school!'

Cow bells

'Have I dreamt this, or were there such things as hippy "cow-bells" in the late sixties? I am sure I had a bell slung round my neck (on a long piece of ribbon) during the summer of '68, or '69. I remember running and jumping round the garden to make it "ding" all the time, until my family and the neighbours were sick of hearing it (it then disappeared never to be seen again!). My colleagues at work don't believe me and say I am making it up.'

'I too was the proud owner of a bell. Boy, did I think I was cool! It was about as close as I got to being a hippy.'

'I had one, which I wore proudly with a few flowers in my hair. I thought I was the bee's knees trotting up to the village shops with it going "tinkle tinkle"! I still have it! How sad can one person get!?'

Grolsch Bottle Tops

'Did anyone else wear Doc Martens with Grolsch Bottle tops through the laces?'

'I had them, I was a big Bros fan. I had the rips in the jeans and also had a leather jacket which I put the Bros logo on and even had a ring made up with Bros on.'

'I remember drinking four bottles of Grolsch so my daughter could have the bottle tops. I can't stand lager and felt like puking after finishing the last one. The landlord then came out with a load of tops when he realised why I wanted them. "You should have asked me for some," he said. Aaaaaaargh!'

Hot pants

'I had a pair of red velvet hot pants. Trouble is, they had a bib, which meant you had to take the damn things off before you could go to the loo!'

Afghans & Love Beads

'My husband remembers walking down the road wearing his sleeveless Afghan waistcoat, tie-dyed cheesecloth shirt and loon jeans covered with love beads. To finish off, he had no shoes on and thought he was Bob Dylan (he was 13 years old) – what a prat, eh!!'

'In 1974–75 (before knee-lengths came in), I lived out in Germany and my school uniform consisted of: a red pleated mini skirt; a yellow puffed-sleeve, high collar shirt (crimplene) and a pink-red tank top with knee-length socks and black platforms. Wow, did I think I looked good.'

Biba

'My girlfriend (now wife of 35 years) used to drag me down to the original Biba on Kensington Church Street [in London] back in about 1964. I seem to recall that it had a single communal changing room with Western saloon-type swing doors. We poor blokes had trouble dragging our eyes away (or at least not getting caught having a sneaky peek by our girls!).'

'It was my all time favourite place – I still have a little, black, skull cap that I bought in Biba! I have never found any makeup as good as theirs. Their small pots of foundation were the best ever.'

'I remember the Biba shop in Manchester, near St Anne's Square. I thought I was the height of fashion wearing their "Metalic Apple" nail polish when I was 14 – about all I could afford at the time.'

Male 'style' 1960

'Aged 16. Single-breasted, black sports coat with white flecks. Only the bottom button done up. White hanky in top pocket. White shirt with cuffs showing. "Gold" cufflinks. "Slim Jim" tie with "gold" tie-pin. Black drainpipe jeans with yellow stitching. Light coloured socks. "Winkle picker" pointed shoes highly polished. Knees of jeans also polished to keep black. All catalogue bought and none of it Armani, Gucci etc, but much smarter than modern, casual scruffs.'

White Stilettoes

'Wore them in early sixties. What *did* we look like, with the paper-nylon underskirts under three tiered skirts, with big white plastic belts round our waists, duster coats on top and BIG white handbags? Not to mention the white gloves, beehive hair do, and the Rain-mate in case it rained!'

'I got married in March 1962 and wore white stiletto-heeled shoes with pointed toes. The only problem came when you bent down and the toes creased and curled up.'

'I had all the accessories to match: necklace, bangles, earrings and handbag, not only in white either, but yellow, pink and pale blue. Would I wear them again? Possibly, but only to my school reunion.'

'I remember using white nail varnish to get the scuff marks off the heels.'

Trainers

'I once had a pair of blue Adidas Trimm Trabs and a pair of Nike Omegas and accidentally went into town wearing one of each – must have looked a right prat – got the first bus back home once I realised.'

'What about Woolworth's plimsoles in black and white? You were usually sent to school with a pair at the beginning of term, only to "accidently" lose them and talk your folks into buying you some Reebok Pump trainers.'

Worst Fashion Disasters

'When I was younger, I thought I was the bee's knees in luminous pink skirt and matching blouse, with those luminous yellow towelling socks.'

'I was very small for my age and couldn't buy adult clothes to fit (at 14), and kids' ones were just ... well kids' clothes. So I made my own. I bought one pattern and adapted it into many wonderful(!) designs. I had a wide range of "bell" shaped dresses – very short (1971). They had long sleeves which were bell shaped or elasticated (great). My favourite was a dark blue one. I sewed white daisy braid around the hem, sleeve edges and neckline ... I even had a matching choker! Even worse: I made some bibbed hot pants – that was OK. But my friend (a very big girl) had matching ones (in the same fabric)... we must have been a sight!'

'I loved pedal pushers – I think I wore them with my RELAX T-shirt! I also used to wear loads of silver bangles during my "gothic" period.'

'Ra-ra skirts and dresses ... we looked like we were wearing a lampshade. Why didn't our partners at the time tell us that these were not at all sexy...?'

'It has to be the Oxford Bags – we used to put tartan down the side when the Bay City Rollers were on the go. That, coupled with the platforms with three-inch soles and five-inch heels and the college jumper!'

'Did anyone have a pair of shoes with three-inch soles? I used to play football in mine!'

'A tartan kilt (complete with big safety pin!) and an Adam Ant frilly blouse! Oh God! I am so ashamed!'

'When I was 12, I wore red-white-and-blue sandals, red-and-white stripey socks and checked three-quarter-length trousers... *and* to top it all off: a gypsy scarf! I looked like an explosion in a paint factory!'

'When they were all the rage I used to wear coloured tights to match the rest of my outfit. If there was blue in my blouse, blue tights; if a sweater had red in it, red tights. I also had yellow, green, purple and orange. Oh the shame.'

Old Perfumes

'Does anyone remember Ambush and Tabu perfumes that we used to wear in the sixties? We sprayed so much of that stuff on us on a Friday and Saturday night, it's a wonder we still don't smell like it after all these years!'

'We boys had to wear Brut, we thought it was so sophisticated.'

'I can remember lots of girls wore Brut as well. On a Friday night at the Top Rank in Bristol that was all you could smell.'

'I used to wear Pagan by Picot and Lady Manhattan by Max Factor. If I close my eyes and take a good sniff, I can still smell them now.'

'I remember a boy I was going out with in the sixties wore Hai Karate. I must have found it appealing at the time!'

'Male perfume in the 1960s: lashings of aftershave, Old Spice and cheaper. Sister's (or mother's) perfumed talc and eau de cologne from a bottle with a rubber thing to squeeze. Otherwise just raw "maleness"!'

The Best Years Of Our Lives

It's been some time since the unkind adage 'If you can't do, teach' held any water. We seem to agree now that teachers do a thankless job, and in some cases shape young lives for the better. They can be mentors, even heroes, offering a moral compass for the life ahead. Having said that, it's often easier, more fun and in some cases cathartic, to remember the bad ones; the tyrants, the monsters, the sadists; the dodgy hairpieces, the stupid catch-phrases, the beastly punishments. The least FriendsReunited can do is offer a forum for sharing memories of past masters; at boot, it can truly exorcise the demons of the past. Was he/she really that bad? Actually, yes. Without skating too close to libel (the message boards had to be taken down for two months once, remember), here are a handful of scholastic memories that will fill your nostrils with the smell of chalk dust and cricket pads. Incidentally, for the sake of balance, you will also hear about a group of inspirational PE teachers along the way, so forget the adjunct, 'If you can't teach, teach gym.'

School's Out

I have managed to contact four of my school pals from Upper Thomas Street, and three from my secondary school (Vicarage Road Secondary Modern) via FriendsReunited and as we are all now pensioners, that's quite a success (well, I think so anyway), and we have quite a cheerful correspondence going. Although two of them are not actually on the Internet we have contacted each through various friends of friends.

I was an 'Upper Thommo kid' (Upper Thomas Street Junior & Infants, Aston). I started there in 1942 and left in 1948 to go to Vicarage Road Secondary Modern Girls School. But ... Upper Thomas Street!

Hands up all those who remember the teacher from Hell? She scared the living daylights out of most of us kids. I can only liken her to the teacher in Dennis Potter's *The Singing Detective* – but she was an old softy compared to my teacher.

I had the disadvantage of being a complete numbskull where sums were concerned – and the particular cross that I had to bear was long division. I couldn't get it, and would have sleepless nights dreading the next arithmetic lesson, thinking when The Evil One would home in on me, and screech and punch me in the back. Of course, this never had the desired effect, but rather sent me into panic mode.

My parents knew that I was having difficulties, and so got some help for me which was fine while I was being tutored, but it all went out of the proverbial window once I was in class. They were unaware of the problems I was having with my tormentor.

I endured all this, without letting on to my mum, because I knew that she would not have been well pleased that her precious daughter was being bullied by this woman. (I should clarify that statement: my mother waited a long time to have me, 13 years, and she and my dad adored me. I would never have admitted that as a child, but with age I can understand their protectiveness of me. That's not to say that I was a spoilt child. No, they did their best to make sure that I was able to stand on my own two feet, and I always had to earn the things that I wanted. Other than at birthday and Christmas of course.)

My other failing at school, was that I was terrible giggler, this did not go down at all well with this teacher; she would run along the rows of desks, and grab me by the scruff of my neck, or jumper or whatever, and punch me all the way to the front of the class. This was a great mystery to my mother, who could never understand why my woollens were always a couple of sizes larger at night than when I had gone to school in them in the morning (always reverting to size after washing). However, my tormentor was the one who gave the game away.

One day my mother called to see if I might leave school a few minutes early, as she had to get the tram into town and it was important that we got there on time. I don't know the details, but no matter. That afternoon had been a particularly difficult one for me, and when my mother arrived she could see that I was upset (my eyes were red and puffy). My teacher was quick to admit (with some pride) that she had found it necessary to thrash me. Oh – My – God! My mum's wrath was a sight to behold. I was terrified that she was going to attack my teacher. (She just about managed to keep herself in check.) I don't know which I was more worried about: the possibility of my mum's attacking her, or the fact that I had to go to school next day and face the woman.

I never did seem to have as much trouble with this teacher after that, although it was an experience that I could well have done without. She carried on with the bullying, but not of me, and also got lots of visits from other pupils' mums (and sometimes dads).

She was the only fly in the ointment of otherwise very happy schooldays at Upper Thomas Street. But that could be another story. I have left out this teacher's name – for the sole reason that I truly do believe that my schoolmates will recognise her by my description and her actions.

However, in the most unlikely possibility that she is still alive, she will know who she is!

Dorothy Dodson (née Sheargold), Prestatyn, North Wales

Up The Hill And Down The Slope

My brother and I were placed in a boarding school in Totteridge in 1941. We stayed there for three years until my parents moved to Oxford and took us back to live with them. I came to Australia at the age of 18 and have been here mostly ever since.

The boarding school experience was a devastating one for both of us, and has had a serious effect on our lives. I am now a writer and ex-journalist and I have written quite a lot about the school and our experiences there.

The Second World War affected many of us who were small children at the time. My brother and I, aged two and four, were originally evacuated with our mother to the countryside and were billeted in various houses. That seems to have worked for a while because my mother's two sisters were also in the same village. One by one they drifted back to London, taking the children with them. My mother became lonely and depressed at having to live in the houses of stangers who, she felt, did not treat her well. She followed her sisters back to London, found herself a job and placed us in The Hill School as boarders.

We did not fare well under this arrangement. I imagine we both thought she had abandoned us forever. My younger brother clung to me as his four-year-old mother. The women who ran the school behaved like tyrants and bullies; the hairbrush was used frequently on our bottoms; children were ritually humiliated and punished by being locked in shoe cupboards and having their wet sheets tied around their necks as a punishment. I remember one teacher telling me frequently I would be hung for murder because I had thick black eyebrows which, at that time, met in the middle.

I believe it wasn't uncommon for English people in a position of power to behave in this tyrannical manner towards children then – read Rudyard Kipling's accounts of his incarceration at a boarding house by the seaside.

However I decided I wanted to find the boarding school a couple of years ago. Local libraries had never heard of it; I tried to contact various local historians but failed to even get a response from any of them. Then I tried advertising in the *Barnet Times* and someone who had been to the school ten years after me saw the ad and contacted me via e-mail. We have been corresponding ever since; furthermore, we added the school, which no longer exists, to the FriendsReunited site and that attracted many other unfortunates who had been sent there – mostly long after my brother and I had left. After all, we were only five and seven when we left.

Now The Hillbillies, as they call themselves, have reunions a couple of times a year. This year I will be visiting England for the first time in 40 years so I can attend a reunion for the first time. I will also be doing some filming of the old place and the ex pupils.

Pip James, Australia

Mother Eleanor

I was messing about on my computer when I came across FriendsReunited. Intrigued I followed the instructions and eventually discovered my old school, St Anthony's, Lewiston Manor, in Dorset, and found myself overwhelmed by emotion.

My father worked for the Foreign Office and my twin sister and I were sent away to boarding school when we were nine years old. Subsequently, the communists in Tsingtao captured my parents and my brother in 1949. They were held under house arrest, so we were effectively orphaned and we did not see them until we were 14 years old. During that time we lived at St Anthony's during term time and at St Mary's, a holiday home for children whose parents were abroad.

My life at the school was dominated by, as far as I was concerned, a bitter, vindictive nun called Mother Eleanor. She had special victims and I was one of them. All of us were expected sycophantically to serve Mother Eleanor's every whim.

I despised her and her lickspittle version of religion. At one point, I was forced to spend all my free time studying in the library. I had to take my meals outside the dining room and wash up with the little sisters after every meal. No one was allowed to talk to me. I was a pariah. My only consolation was my best friend Kate, whom Mother Eleanor also persecuted. Years later, when I was running a refuge, I wrote my memoir called *Infernal Child*. It described in great detail Mother Eleanor's cruelty and I sent her a copy.

I was deeply scared by Mother Eleanor's hatred of me. She thought I was stupid and lazy. In fact, I am seriously dyslexic, and although the condition was unknown in those days, there was little excuse for Mother Eleanor to torment and humiliate those of us she considered recalcitrant pupils. Kate and a few other friends were a consolation to me and I was always sorry that I lost touch with Kate when I married and left England.

I posted a vituperative account of my relationship with Mother Eleanor on the FriendsReunited site and forgot about the whole incident. Several weeks later, I got e-mail from Alice Rae. She said her mother had often talked about me as her best friend at school and would I like to contact her on her e-mail? I was delighted. Finally, I had found Kate. I e-mailed her and made arrangements to visit her in Bridport. Alice had a friend who worked on the *Daily Express* and he liked the story of our about-to-be historic meeting and offered to come and take pictures for the newspaper.

Driving down to Bridport, I felt a huge sense of nostalgia. Kate, it turned out, lives a few yards away from St James' Secretarial College where I spent a year's incarceration learning to be the world's worst secretary. St Mary's Holiday Home, where I was supremely happy, was only 20 or so miles away in Uplyme and I felt I was coming home.

My first novel, *The Watershed*, was all set in this countryside and when I finally found this beautiful little cottage, I saw Kate standing outside and nothing had changed. I recognised her immediately, even though some 40 years had elapsed since we'd seen each other. Oblivious to the photographer, we hugged each other and the words fell out of my mouth.

'Do you remember Mother Eleanor?' Kate's outraged snort made me collapse with laughter. She did indeed and we talked for hours.

The *Express* printed a picture and the story of our reunion and I got a call from another national newspaper. Would I like to contact a few of my friends from school and the newspaper would pay for us to meet in London and have a slap-up lunch? The journalist said the newspaper was really so excited by the idea of the story that they were also going to provide a makeup artist plus find designer clothes. Finally, a very famous photographer would take photographs for the shoot and we would each be given a souvenir photograph to take home. It sounded like fun and a chance to catch up on old friends.

I telephoned my old school to find that the nuns were no longer there and Mother Eleanor died a while ago. A huge cloud lifted off my shoulders. She could no longer harm other children at the school. I was also aware from e-mails I received from women who'd seen the *Express* article and who had been at St Anthony's that Mother Eleanor was seen by some as a devil but by others as a saint. Those she chose not to persecute had very happy memories of her, but I also had many disturbing e-mails from women like myself who had bitter and often very traumatic memories of her emotionally violent behaviour.

The school could not have been more helpful and gave me a list of contacts and I set out to find Mary Rose, Georgina and Jill. Mary Rose was a brilliant student and a school rebel. She had huge green eyes, enormous eyelashes and black hair. She features in many of my novels as an adventurer. Georgina was the school's 'golden girl'.

Everyone loved Georgina and I passionately wished I could be like her. Jill was a steadying influence and ended up as a head girl of the school. How much would they have changed?

Kate and I spent many phone calls wondering about the meeting. I was to produce photographs of us when we were at school together. I managed to find one, but promptly lost it. The journalist was not pleased, but I promised to find other copies and, after talking to the other four, we cobbled together various photographs that showed us sitting in rows looking steadfastly into a school camera and the innocence in our faces was heartbreaking. What would we all look like now?

Mary Rose had a fashionable streak of grey in her dark locks. She had become an entrepreneur and was now going to have horses to fulfil a lifetime ambition. She of all of us, I thought, had changed the least. Georgina still had that ineffable light about her face and the same sweet smile. She had five children and made her home and her family her life.

Kate was married to an excellent artist and also ran business ventures, especially a very successful clothing business. Jill was a top-flight businesswoman. We all had children and only Jill and myself were divorced.

We arrived at the restaurant in Chelsea to discover it was a very sixties coffee shop with holes in the ceiling. The journalist apologised, but fortunately we were too excited to care. The years fell away and we were 16 again.

My slight worry was the idea of the designer clothes for the photo shoot, as I am outsize, but the journalist reassured me that it was all in hand. We had been informed that the managing director of this newspaper did not allow women to wear trousers for this sort of story. Georgina was not happy because she had planned to wear a trouser suit, but in deference to the great man's edict we were all be-skirted.

The meal was truly awful, but the conversation was fantastic. In a fit of remorse the journalist rushed off to buy two bottles of champagne.

We were poured into taxis and taken to the photo shoot. Here disappointment loomed large. The organiser was suffering from acute toothache and the 'designer clothes' were largely unpacked and lying in carrier bags on the floor. The makeup girl was chatty, but we all felt the results were terrible and, just before we were to be photographed, we were told that we would have to be stripped of any jewellery including our watches because the great man did not approve of women wearing jewellery in his photographs. True to form, Kate and I went on strike and I refused to remove my cross. We stood in a circle after being ordered to make like the television show *Friends* and the 'famous' photographer stood on top of a ladder and snapped away.

The occasion proved to be very disappointing and a little humiliating, but our meeting with each other was a marvellous event and left all of us happy and grateful to FriendsReunited. Needless to say the journalist insisted that the reason that the piece was not printed was because I could not provide one photograph with all of us in it. But as far as we were concerned, we had a wonderful time and we are now able to be in touch with each other.

I think FriendsReunited does a magnificent job in a world that is largely fragmented by allowing people to reconnect and find each other. For me, it was very cathartic to find old friends and to discover that Mother Eleanor's long shadow was cast over other children not just myself. Kate and I were not some sort of freaks – Mother Eleanor was the problem.

The only blessing she brought me was that years later when I was fighting to keep the refuge open against terrific opposition, my experiences of her sadistic bullying helped me survive. She couldn't break me when I was a defenceless child and therefore when I faced repeated attempts to jail me I was able to endure.

© **Erin Pizzey, author and founder of the first women's refuge, London**

Pass The Salt

It was 1946. I was just four years old and it was my first day at school in Mossley, Lancashire. I was having my dinner at school and I was putting some salt on my roast beef when the top came off and the whole lot landed on my plate. I didn't know what to do, so I mixed it into my dinner to hide it. Then the teacher came along, and realising I wasn't eating anything urged me to 'Eat up, that's a good girl'.

She stood there until I, with tears running down my cheeks, ate every horrible mouthful. I was too little to explain what had happened. I spent the rest of the day in misery.

Norma Kershaw, Brisbane, Australia

Howzat?

I was astonished one evening when my PE Teacher, Mr Kevin Maloney, approached me and said, 'O' Connell, bring your whites in tomorrow – you'll be needing them as you will be playing cricket with us at Richmond.'

The match was being played between Barnes & Richmond Teachers and London Transport. Not being a teacher but a 13-year-old pupil at Cardinal Manning, I was what is today referred to as a 'ringer'.

I owed much of my sporting education to Mr Kevin Maloney, but in the cricket department Mr E Nelson was excellent and joined the lads during the lunch hours from time to time to train and help us out.

The day arrived, as did I with my whites. Nervous, I sat in the back of Mr Nelson's car on the way to Richmond Green, where we changed in the Cricketers' Public House which was very aptly named. I bowled and took two wickets plus a handful of runs while batting. After the match, which we won, we all walked back to the Cricketers' to change. Having changed and collected my kit bag, I thanked every one for the game, but could not see Mr Maloney or Mr Doyle.

To leave the Cricketers' pub I had to make my way downstairs and walk through the bar. Having reached the bar, I saw Mr Maloney and Mr Doyle drinking their respective pints at the bar. I approached them and thanked them for the game. They replied, 'That's all right, Michael, thanks for coming.'

As I reached for the door to leave the premises, Mr Maloney screamed out (for Richmond, I think), 'O'Connell! Come here lad!' He went on: 'You deem to leave these premises after we've given you a game of cricket... and you're not even going to buy Mr Doyle and myself a pint!'

'Well, sir,' I replied, 'I have only got my bus fare to get home.' I reached deep into my pockets and with some justification, took out my meagre coins.

'Put that away, son,' said Mr Maloney and, turning to the publican, 'Pull the lad a pint!'

I hadn't eaten since lunch time and the pint went straight to my head.

This is indicative of the kindness teachers gave to pupils at Cardinal Manning. Many of them came from Strawberry Hill College and were fine professional men.

[I dedicate this story to Mr A Doyle; Mr E Nelson; Mr K Maloney – forever my mentors in sport.]

Mike O'Connell

Revenge

When I was at school I was caned by the headmaster, Mr Jennings (somewhat unnecessarily I thought), for failing to do my homework.

I got my own back, though ...

He used to park his car, a maroon Wolsley 1300 saloon, near a bike shed, which was just behind the school kitchen, where we used to hide for a cigarette in the lunch hour.

One day, a delivery of spuds had been made and one of the bags had split. Using the handle of a brush (from a brush and pan set left in a doorway), I poked a dozen or more potatoes up the exhaust pipe. I think I must have filled the rear silencer box!

The head's car would only run for a second or two and then the engine would stop. It was left there for the best part of a week and eventually had to be towed away! Hah hah!!

Dave Warrillow

Miss G

We nailed a rotten kipper under her desk and she took two hours to find it –
by then we were all feeling sick.

(Appeared on a Message Board)

Mr P

Our English teacher. As the term went on, his hair would get greyer and
greyer. Then, after the hols, he would come back with fantastic black hair
again! He must have been in his sixties, which made it funnier.

(Appeared on a Message Board)

Mr M

Remember his wig? Someone said it fell in his soup whilst he was in the
school canteen.

(Appeared on a Message Board)

Mr M

He was possibly the best ever maths teacher, placating restless students on
the last day of winter term by bringing in his electric guitar and strumming
the following:

1. 'Stairway to Heaven'
2. 'Money For Nothing'

Seemed pretty cool at the time, and despite much begging (and pencil-cases
being thrown out of windows), he never did it again.

(Appeared on a Message Board)

A Punishment With Balls

In the third year at Boteler Grammar School, I, Bob (Fred) Fretwell, and (I think) Ian (Blob) Lomax of 5B received a fitting punishment!

It had been snowing in 1958 and a thick covering of snow was spread around the grounds. Ian and I spent part of our lunch break spelling out the words 'The Oaf' by sticking snowballs onto the school's back wall. We were about to return to our classes when who should be standing there but Mr Forsythe, known to one and all by the nickname (you guessed it!) 'The Oaf'.

'Very artistic, boys,' he said, and I swear he had the glimmer of a previously unused grin. 'Before you come back into class, I'd like to see, in the same size letters, please, the words "Merry Christmas Mr Forsythe".'

It was FREEZING! By the time we had returned to the classroom for our belated French lesson our hands were blue (those letters were two feet high)! Mr Forsythe didn't bat an eyelid. 'Ah! Come in, boys, get out your books.'

Not a cross word, no 'caning' (as was the norm then) – in fact, never another word was said about the incident. But over the years, I have often reflected on that exquisite and perfect punishment. That was the last year I took French, but he will live on in my brain as an example! I'm 60 next birthday, so 'The Oaf' is probably not with us any longer, but if he's watching, I'd like him to know he left his mark!

Bob Fretwell

There is a certain logic to the way children look at the world. (Well there ought to be – it's adults that tell them most of this guff!)

'I always believed that sheep that lived on hillsides were a special breed that had two legs shorter than the others and that dark-skinned ladies used cocoa powder as makeup (thanks Dad!). Please tell me I wasn't alone? I know better now.'

'My dad told my brother that he was Superman, but it was a secret. My brother spent many a happy hour searching for the suit, which was supposedly hidden in a suitcase under the bed. (I guess he didn't find it because it was magic!) Personally, I'm rather glad he didn't find hidden tights belonging to my dad …'

'I lived next to Shaw Lane cricket ground in Barnsley when I was a kid, and they had a sign saying "Trespassers will be prosecuted". I thought "prosecuted" was the same as "exterminated", like the Daleks. I have never set foot in Shaw Lane to this day.'

'My mum used to say, "David your bedroom looks like a bomb's hit it!" But I thought "a bomb's hit it" was all one word meaning a mess, e.g. "looks like a right *bomsitit*", or "You look a bit of a bomsitit".'

'They told me that my toys came to life when I was asleep. I spent many a night attempting to spot this happening.'

'Thunder storms were God having a spring clean.'

'My dad told me that we had belly buttons because babies were baked in an oven and God prodded them to see if they were done. He spun me this whole story about God going along the production line saying. "You're done, you're done". Well, it stopped me asking questions for a few years!'

'My mum used to tell me that babies were ordered from the supermarket and when she had my brother and went into hospital, she told me that her order was ready and she had to go and collect him.'

What was your favourite toy when you were a child, or did you just make your own entertainment?

'A Compendium of Games was the standard Christmas present from one of your relations. I received one nearly every year through the fifties. There were probably around eight board type games in one box: ludo, draughts, snakes and ladders, lotto etc.'

'Does anyone remember the glow-in-the-dark models made by Aurora? I used to scare the daylights out of my brother with them all – Dracula, Frankenstein, the Creature from the Black Lagoon etc.'

'I found a book in the children's library that gave instructions on how to make a weak version of nitro-glycerine!! The solution was mixed wet then newspaper was soaked in it. You then rolled the wet newspaper up into little balls and put them on the floor to dry. If someone stood on them when dry, they made a sharp crack. The book did say that under no circumstances should any of the balls be larger than half an inch as it could be dangerous! And this was in the children's library! It told you how to make gunpowder too!'

'Did anyone have a crystal radio? I got one for Christmas when just a nipper. My dad strung up a 100-foot aerial from my bedroom window to the clothes-line pole at the end of the garden. The BBC's Light Programme came in loud and clear.'

'Jennifer, next door, had an older brother, Clive. He and I used his chemistry set to make fireworks (highly illegal), which we did very carefully. We used to make very successful Roman candles that shot out different coloured flares. The tubes were fashioned from newspaper soaked in wallpaper paste and wrapped onto a broomstick. Our smaller fireworks were made in cigar tubes.'

'My brother had a papier-mâché sword and, of course, the usual cowboy cap guns. He also had a toy gun which looked like a German Luger pistol and was actually stopped by the police when he was about nine years old so they could check it was only a toy!'

'In the late forties and early fifties, I remember playing outside on bombsites. This involved making houses out of one layer of bricks, and using roof slates as plates for dinner, picking weeds to use as the vegetables! We would pair up with the boys to be our husbands and play mums and dads – oh, so innocent!'

'My cat fitted into my doll's dresses and hats. I used to get told off for doing it, but the cat always came back for more!'

'I can remember tying my brother's leg up behind his back so he could be Long John Silver. We didn't have a stick to use though for a peg leg, so he had to lean against the wall saying "Aaarrgh, Jim lad", and not moving. Come to think of it, he didn't have a parrot on his shoulder either.'

'I did put mum's false teeth (top and bottom set) in one day when I was about four and it took ages to get them back out. Mum had a visitor at the time and was most embarrassed as I walked in with the teeth in looking horrendous and said, "I'sh got mum's falsh teesh in." I was in loadsa trouble.'

"I seem to remember little paper flowers, all strung together, that you put in a glass of water and they opened out and made a garden: these were beautiful, but my fear is that they were only a figment of my imagination.'

'I remember toys that walked down a slope or board. You could get animals, as well as people, all made of plastic. Pluto, and Mickey Mouse were the ones I had. They sort of wobbled and fell if the slope was too steep – very popular little toys – and were available for many years. Came on to the scene from the 1940s onwards.'

'I belonged to the News Chronicle I-Spy Club. You bought a little paper book on one or other of a variety of subjects (anything from railways to wildflowers) and went spotting. My favourite was the one on different car models. You scored points depending on how rare the car model was and once the book was filled in your parents authenticated it. You then sent it in and got a coloured feather from Hawkeye and the status of a brave. A full head dress made you a chief.'

Fame!

Just to prove that everyone has to go to school at some point, even if they do end up as the most famous person on the planet, here are stories from members of FriendsReunited who can recall the great and the good before they achieved their 15 minutes (or more) of fame

Stephanie Beacham
Queen Elizabeth's Grammar School for Girls, High Street, Barnet, Herts

In my first year at QEGGS, I distinctly remember sitting behind Steph in our classroom. We were talking about what we wanted to do when we left school and Stephanie turned round and said, in a very determined manner, 'Well I'm going to be a famous actress.'

Delia Smith
Bexleyheath Secondary Modern School For Girls, Bexleyheath

I remember her well. She won the first prizes in decorating cakes etc in cookery. She looks no different now to when she was at school (she has hardly aged at all) – well done, Delia.

Twiggy (Lesley Hornby)
Bridge Road County Primary, Bridge Road, Church End, Willesden

She and I were both members of Miss Downer's recorder group. Funny how she has never mentioned that on any of her TV appearances!

Leigh Lawson
Templars School

In the Junior School one day I was asked to stand up and read aloud. I was quiet then and very shy. I hesitated and the boy next to me stood up and encouraged me. A few years later, my brother Philip became friendly with this boy, Alan, and often brought him to our house. Alan had always wanted to become an actor and his family moved to Stratford-upon-Avon to give his career a chance. He later changed his name to Leigh Lawson and met Twiggy to whom he is now married. **(Tina Peake)**

Steve Pankhurst
Orange Hill, Burnt Oak, Edgware
Surprised no one's added him. Probably one of OH's more successful pupils …

Karen (now Jessie) Wallace (Kat from *EastEnders*)
Ambrose Fleming School, Hertford Road, Enfield, Middlesex
Ah, I have fond memories of Karen… I remember her and me being suspended because of fighting in the teachers' car park… Ah well, at least I kicked her ass!

David Puttnam
Minchenden School, High Street, Southgate, London N14
Tall, slim, quiet lad two to three years ahead of me. His father, if I remember rightly, owned a camera shop and David always had one at school, which we used to borrow to take pics of our current 'crush' on sports days! Most of the teachers said he would never do anything.

Eric Bristow
Hackney Downs, Hackney, E London
The 'Crafty Cockney' darts maestro. I remember being called upon to 'remove' him from the library once, when he and his gang were wrecking it.

Royston Langdon
Abbey Grange Church of England High School, Leeds
I went to school with a guy called Royston Langdon. We were in the same class and quite friendly. Well, he has made it huge in America with a band called Spacehog and recently married Liv Tyler, the actress from *Lord of the Rings*.
(Linzi Renolds, née Wright)

Michael Caine
Hackney Downs, (Hackney, E London)
Maurice Micklewhite was from South London, but was evacuated during the War to King's Lynn to stay with a relative – his aunt, I think. However, the nearest grammar school, King Edward VII, did not have room for him and suggested that he join the other.

Sue Barker
Marist Convent School, Fulham Road, SW10
She went to Marist and was given tennis lessons by Sister Catherine, who also let us watch all Ms Barker's matches when Wimbledon was on!

Simon Le Bon
Pinner Grammar School, Beaulieu Drive, Pinner, Middlesex
He wanted to join our band, Lear, but was considered too podgy. I painted one of the pillars in the art room, while he worked on the one next to it, and remember thinking him quite unremarkable. Truth is stranger than fiction …

Eric Blair (George Orwell)
Fray's College, Harefield Road, Uxbridge, Middlesex
Eric Blair joined school as a teacher from Hayes at the end of 1933. He went on to become the well-known George Orwell. I heard that most of staff lived in and there was a no-smoking rule laid down by the Principal, but this was ignored by Eric Blair!

Rod Stewart
Chiswick Polytechnic Technical School, Chiswick, London
Yes — the very one. He was there in my brother's class, doing O Levels!! He had already started his musical career and played at Eel Pie Island, Twickenham with Long John Baldry.

Stanley Baker
Riverside Academy, Ferndale Junior School, Rhondda
My mother, Mary Georgina Davies (née Caudle) attended school with the actor Stanley Baker. He used to watch slides provided by my grandfather on the magic lantern, little realising that he himself would appear on such a silver screen.
(Ann Davies)

Chris Britton
Andover Grammar School
I remember Chris Britton who later became a member of The Troggs. 'Wild Thing' was their first number one hit in about 1965 or '66. If my memory serves me correctly, he used to play classical guitar and often gave impromptu performances at school dances and parties, but I don't remember him every playing a piece all the way through!
(Pauline Cadogan)

Lenny Henry
St John's, Birmingham
I remember Lenny Henry being in my class at St John's. He was always getting into trouble with our then class teacher Mr Edwards. I seem to remember his dad coming to the school once and having a good go at Mr Edwards in the corridor while we all listened.

Robert Plant (Led Zeppelin)
King Edward VI, Stourbridge
I caught the same bus as him and shared my first fag of the day. Then at break-time behind the bike shed we shared another smoke and he said his ambition was 'to play the harmonica in the back streets of Chicago'.

Melanie Brown (Spice Girls)
Kirkstall School, Kirkstall Road, Leeds
I remember walking home for lunch with her a couple of times. She was a popular girl then, too. Imagine my surprise to see her on *Top of the Pops* years later!

Jack Straw
Leeds University
President of Students' Union c. 1968 — a good year for sit-ins. Was not amused at a debate when a group of fellow students tried to remove his trousers and puncture his pomposity.

Fred 'Fiery' Truman
Maltby Hall Secondary Modern School, Braithwell Road, Maltby
Fred was reputed to be the fastest bowler in the history of cricket. I know, as I was one of many who faced him at school. Unfortunately, he was severely injured at school when, I believe, he sustained a rupture, but won his way back to greatness by sheer willpower.

Julie Christie
Wycombe Court School, Lane End, Nr High Wycombe
Nickname at school 'Bugs', she was good fun.

Rick Wakeman
Drayton Manor Grammar School, Hanwell, Middlesex

Rick Wakeman was in the year below me. He had real musical talent even then and the school organ took a bashing from him. It was traditional for the Sixth Form to perform some kind of entertainment for the rest of the school just before leaving and we staged *Sleeping Beauty*. He played the 'Sleeping Beauty Waltz' off key throughout the show!

(Sandra Hart)

All Around The World

Australia, New Zealand, Canada, Malaysia, Germany, Essex – here's where FriendsReunited proves the old cliché, 'It's a small world'. Nobody seems to call the Internet the 'worldwide web' any more, despite the ubiquity of the 'www' prefix. Perhaps that's because it's a slightly naff alliterative phrase. And maybe we've actually started to become blasé about the fact that the click of a modem can connect us to any point in the wired world within seconds. FriendsReunited maintains its local feel thanks to the abiding notion of Steve and Julie Pankhurst in their Barnet semi, but it's very much a global concern now, and has already helped find people who have emigrated to the other side of the world. No matter where you live now, if you attended, say, Warnham Court Boarding School in Sussex, you have an instant link with the past. Many of these stories involve hands across the ocean, travelling back to the place where you went to school or spent your formative years, and the way the miles just shrink away. Clicking the heels on your red slippers and saying, 'There's no place like home,' is no longer necessary.

Our House

I received an e mail not long after I had registered with FriendsReunited from a girl I vaguely remembered from my junior school. She remembered my brother and me because my mum had taught her, and she was interested to hear how my mum was keeping and catch up with our news.

I e mailed her back with our news. She is now living in New Zealand and is a teacher herself, so it was interesting to compare her life with ours. We corresponded quite frequently and I actually traced a girl for her that she had lost touch with who was living close to me.

In one of our e-mails, she mentioned the street where she used to live when she was at junior school. Funnily enough, it happens to be the street where I live with my family now. I mentioned this to her the next time I corresponded and told her which number we live at.

Can you believe it ... my friend used to live here in this very house!

To prove this, when we were recently redecorating my daughter's bedroom we stripped right down to the original wall and found my friend's mum's signature and date on the wall we were papering.

Beverley Harrison (née Simpson), Ulverston, Cumbria

Neighbours

I had emigrated to Australia in 1987 and through time and because of the distance had lost contact with many old school chums, especially one friend, Trevor. I had been trying to find him for many years; we are now in our late forties.

I was pleasantly surprised to find his name on FriendsReunited.

I returned to the UK to try and catch up with him and a few others that I had lost contact with. It had been 17 years since my emigration and I was not full of much expectation of finding him. I knew he was alive because his name was on the school list, but I didn't know where he lived. I just hoped he still lived in Plymouth.

Whilst staying with my mother, I decided one day to try the local telephone directory, and to my surprise he was still living in Plymouth. Picking up the phone, I dialled the number. A woman answered and I cautiously asked if Trevor Kenward was available. After explaining that I was an old school friend and not to say anything because I wanted to surprise him, I waited.

Glancing down at the book, I received another surprise. With phone in hand, I walked out of my mother's front door, turned right at the end of the path and proceeded (still talking to him on the phone), to walk 20 yards or so up the road.

Ringing the door bell of the house two doors away from my mother, I heard him ask me if I could hang on because someone was at the door. I could hear him walking up the stairs, about half way up the stairs, a voice came back over the phone: 'You're bloody standing at my front door, aren't you?'

The door opened, and there we stood, still with phones in hand.

The chances of that have to be one in several million.

Kevin Kerslake, Melbourne, Australia

Oh Carole

I emigrated to New Zealand from England in 1973, and three years later my friend Carole decided to save up to come and see me. Her mother and some of her colleagues, were persuaded to invest in stamps by a very plausible gentleman who worked with them. It was intended that the proceeds be used for Carole to fly to New Zealand; we were highly excited. Then, on 10 January 1977, Carole sent me a letter, which made it feel like the bottom had fallen out of our world. To quote her:

'This man appeared to know a lot about stamps, and said if anyone had any stamps he'd take them and have them auctioned – he'd make a profit and so would we. After a while, all the members of his investment club got about £50 from stamps they'd sold. This made us all believe in him and so we decided to sell our first day covers, which we'd collected over the last few years. He reckoned on us getting £212 for each one, which was marvellous. However, it appears he was not all he made out to be – he promised people money which they never got. Some of the staff even paid him money (thousands of pounds in some cases) for stamps which he'd then auction. They didn't see any money... we're beginning to wonder if he's a crook ...'

Her fears were well-founded, and the 'gentleman' later ended up residing 'at her Majesty's pleasure' on similar offences, I believe. Their money was never recovered.

It then took until Christmas Eve 2002 for Carole finally to make the trip; this time with her younger daughter, who was the age we were when the first trip was planned! We had an amazing nine days together (all she could manage as a busy teacher on leave), and still loved each other's company.

Shared memories of school days at Sunnymede Infants and Junior School (Billericay, Essex) revolved a lot around teachers and activities.

We'd started together on my first day at school in 1965 when she was asked to look after me. We used to be in plays together – she was Snow White to my Grumpy!

We played clapping games: 'Under the brambles, under the sea. True love for you my darling, true love for me. When we are married, we'll raise a family. Boy for you. Girl for me. Umdiddly um dum. Sexy!' (Very risque!) and ran 'clubs' at playtimes, where we sold little things we'd made out of matchboxes etc, then gave the money to charities like Oxfam. We represented the school in the inter-school road safety competition, where we had to learn the Road Code off by heart and answer questions. In the final, my skirt elastic broke just as I had to stand up to answer my question. I managed to hold it up, but my concentration slipped, and we only came second!

Colour TVs were just starting to come out (we had a black and white). I was a foundation member of the Puffin Club (Puffin books) from 1967, and still have all my magazines, which my children now love. I've also used them to stimulate interesting literacy activities for my student teachers and children I've taught.

I tend to be a nostalgic sort of person with a strong interest in history, so my past and the connection to it is really important to me. My siblings don't feel the same though. I'm sure I went into teaching as a career because I'd been lucky to have such great primary teachers myself, and I wanted to pass some of that magic on.

Finding Carole again via FriendsReunited was one of the real highlights of my life, and I went round smiling and telling people about it for weeks. It seemed truly miraculous. There's something intangible yet crucial about connecting with your roots and childhood ... especially from those less stressful days of the sixties and seventies.

Sue Bridges (née Clifford), Christchurch, New Zealand

Jolly And Lucky

Through the site I have once again made contact with a neighbour and friend of 55 years, whom I had not heard from since she emigrated to Canada 43 years ago. We are both now 60, grandmothers, each with a new grandaughter born last year, called Alyssa.

It has been a wonderful experience linking up with Nan Cramsie in Vancouver and catching up gradually with her family news, and establishing again the warm relationship we enjoyed so much as children.

Our favourite game in the late forties was 'Pretend Horse' and we would spend hours galloping around the block in Auchinairn on our two imaginary mounts, Jolly and Lucky.

Nan and I both recalled this game in our first e-mails across the world – our stock phrase was: 'We're jolly lucky to have two horses like Jolly and Lucky'. A bit twee, I guess, but in the days of the *Chalet School* novels quite acceptable.

I have already enjoyed two lovely face-to-face reunions with classmates of the sixties, one who still resides in Glasgow, whilst the other travelled from Switzerland for our lunch date.

Joan Ferguson (née Munro), Banff, Aberdeenshire

Close To You

An old school friend, Margaret Piner, and I were wondering where the third member of our little trio – Betty Pitman – could be. I had not seen her since she left school in 1953. My son suggested I should put my name on FriendsReunited in the vague hope of getting in touch with her.

A couple of weeks later her name appeared, and I e-mailed Betty and the outcome was astounding, to say the least. It would appear she spent 20 years of her first marriage in my village, and was a founder member of our WI to which I belong. When I heard what her surname was I was speechless.

It turns out that her daughter-in-law and my daughter-in-law are sisters, which means our grandchildren are cousins. Her other grandchildren and the grandchildren of our other school friend have played with each other. Also we were at the 60th birthday party of our daughters-in-law's mother and did not even know. When I mentioned her name to the WI ladies so many of them remembered her and were still in touch with her. The last part is that she only lives about ten minutes' journey away from me. We have met up and also had a meal together with two other friends. I never ever thought she would still be in the vicinity, let alone only a short distance away and we had never met!

Heather Ellis (née Mackins), Minster, Nr Ramsgate, Kent

Easy Rider

I have a story about a young German lad of about 18, who came to England on his motorcycle years ago when I was a toddler. He befriended my family on the South Downs of England at a time when Germans were still unpopular, soon after World War II. My father treated him like his son and Heiko became like a big brother in our rapidly growing family (later totalling nine children).

My mother recalls that she and my father first met Heiko when they bailed him out of a sticky spot. Heiko and his friend were caught by a local farmer taking milk from the churn left out for collection at the farm front gate. They were hungry and had no money to eat. This was in the Devon area (where I first started out myself – born in Appledore and living in a gypsy-type caravan built by my dad). Heiko came over on a boat with a young friend of his (a last minute decision), a cargo type to Southampton – motorbike and all. They had no money but a lot of talk persuaded the captain to carry them.

Heiko reminded me of the day when I was about six years old and we were busy in the Dutch Barn attached to the house. Heiko was fixing the motor on his bike and, tomboy that I was, I figured I could be a big help!

The story goes that I was unusually silent for a while and then finally piped up, 'Heiko? How many years older are you than me?'

He answered. I replied: 'Well then – you must wait for me to grow a bit older, then we can get married!!' Baerbel (his wife) tells me she is relieved he did not wait!

My family eventually emigrated to New Zealand when I was 13 years old and Heiko – who thought of us as his own family by then – spent more than 35 years trying to find us again. He and his wife travelled to New Zealand and asked in the schools and parishes where he thought we would be known.

But the timing was wrong – it was holidays and no one at the convent was there. They advertised in the local papers but alas due to false leads were looking in the wrong place.

I returned to the UK with my husband on work assignment with IBM the year before last and by a series of coincidences I was 'found' by the boyfriend of Heiko's daughter on the FriendsReunited site.

We have stayed with him and his wife in Buxtehude, near Hamburg and we really hope that we can see each other again before we have to return home to the other side of the world at the end of July this year. We are also trying to find ways that Heiko and Baerbel can meet the rest of my family who live in Australia and New Zealand.

I really have FriendsReunited to thank big time!!!

Merrily Willis, New Zealand

House Of Windsor

Casually, I glanced down the list of names on my old school details on the FriendsReunited site, and then suddenly stopped dead.

Roger Farrow!!

Could it be the same one? Well ... it had to be. I opened the notes box and there it was: 'Anyone that remembers me? Especially Dan Levey who I used to torment so much ...'

I didn't remember him tormenting me, quite the opposite, in fact. He really looked out for me. I'd have to buy him a drink. Then I read the disappointing line:

'I'm living in Malaysia now...'

My word, I remember all right, seems like yesterday.

I attended Warnham Court boarding school in Sussex. I'd arrived mid term and was allocated a bed in Thrush dormitory, one of the smaller rooms with only five beds. On his bed by the window sat Roger, I wasn't yet wearing the school uniform and he looked at my clothes with interest. I was 13, he was a couple of years older than me. He was a good bit taller and had been around the block a few times.

The first thing he did was to put me right on my tie knot. 'That knot's crap,' he advised. 'Looks like something a girl tied on her gym belt.'

I had to admit it did too.

'See, you need to tie a Windsor knot.'

Hands flashed and within seconds he had a perfectly triangular knot in his tie. He then stood behind me in front of the mirror, his arms over my shoulders while he tied the knot on my tie.

I've always knotted my ties that way ever since. He went on to admire my trousers (tight) but scorned my shoes. 'Winkle-pickers are out,' he said, 'and chisel toes are coming in.'

These things were important to know when you were away from home all term. If you went back looking like a carrot-cruncher, you could lose all your cred in one go. It would be worse than not knowing the words to 'I Guess it Doesn't Matter Any More' by Buddy Holly.

That's how I remember him. Tall, 'been there done that', always happy to make sure you didn't make a prat of yourself – you were in his dorm after all.

So I replied to his message on FriendsReunited and mentioned how disappointed I was that we couldn't get together for a drink. He replied, saying he'd be back for about ten days from 20 February, so we could meet then.

The best laid plans of mice and men. I wasn't too surprised when I didn't hear from him; these flying visits have a way of running out of time.

Monday morning about 9:15 and the telephone rings. It's Roger. He's in the UK and has been trying to ring me all week, but the silly sod has forgotten how to use the telephone. He's been dialling 0 44 in front of the number just as he would in Malaysia.

'Can we meet? If so, it's got to be today.'

'OK,' I say, 'London 2:30.'

I didn't know where to meet him so I suggested Fenchurch Street mainline station. It's the London terminus I get into from Essex but I also knew that it would be fairly deserted in the middle of the day, while the underground stations would be heaving.

'I'll be wearing a black leather jacket,' he said, 'And a tie ... I always wear a tie.'

Nothing changes, Windsor knot and all. I came down the escalator and saw a guy waiting in the doorway. Our eyes locked. It had to be him, but his hair wasn't grey, it was a light brown. From a distance he didn't look old enough. He was leaning back against the wall and as I approached he pulled himself up to his full height.

Jeez, I thought, I could have the wrong guy here. He looked up at me. I'm not tall but this guy was three inches shorter than me. Funny the way everything looks much larger when you're a kid.

'I knew it was you, straight away,' he said. 'Your hair's grey, but your face hasn't changed much.'

We went off into Fenchurch Street and into a pub called the Slug and Lettuce. He produced a pile of old photos from school days and some new ones of his home in Malaysia. We compared all the girls at the school. Every one of them seemed beautiful, God knows why I spurned them back then.

Well, I do know. Any girl you dated had to be third year or fourth year. Anyone younger than that was no-go, regardless of what they looked like. Peer pressure.

I thought the meeting would be difficult but, in fact, the time raced by. We were the only customers and after a while Roger produced his camera and suggested a photograph. I went up to the people standing around watching us from behind the bar.

'You probably think we're a pair of old gays,' I said and they all fell about. 'Could you take our photo, we haven't seen each other for...'

It really was over 44 years. Where did the time go?

The afternoon raced by but oddly, we both seemed to know when it was time to leave. Early evening and the pub was beginning to fill with local businessmen. We headed back in the direction of Fenchurch Street Station. We were both walking slowly – almost shuffling our feet to delay the moment.

Outside the station we stopped, getting under people's feet as they hurried for their trains. An awkward embarrassed moment that men don't handle too well. Probably never see each other again.

'I don't know if I should risk this,' Roger said. I laughed, I was about to say the same. He swung his arm around me and we clung onto each other in a way that we would never have done in the 1950s before 'new man' came along. Briefcases and handbags brushed us as people hurtled past without batting an eye.

We each turned to go and walked in opposite directions. In the doorway I looked back in time to see him disappear around the corner towards Tower Hill and the train that would take him back to his sister's house in Highgate. I was suddenly very weary, my legs were like lead and the stairs to the platform seemed like a mountain.

See, most of my life I'd been frozen in time, somewhere between the going of Buddy Holly and the coming of the Beatles. Meeting an old man had put an end to that. Before we met I thought that one or the other of us would run out of things to say and get bored with the other's company. In fact, that didn't happen. We seemed to reach the conclusion at the same moment that it was time to put the memories back in the box.

All I know now is that I've lived a very long time and it seems like five minutes. We've a reunion planned at the local village hall. The school was a beautiful mansion that was converted into apartments and sold off about four years ago. It's a sore point with the ex-pupils. We'll probably wander around the grounds and annoy the residents.

Dan Levey, Noak Bridge, Essex

California Dreaming

Last August, I had a phone call from a friend, Julie, who lives in San Mateo, California with her husband and two children. She asked me which school I had attended during my teens and in which year did I leave. Cautiously, I enquired why, but she insisted I tell her. When I said St Marylebone Central School in Westminster, in London and that I had left in 1954, she asked me to hang on a second and then asked if I recognised any names from a list that she read out.

Some of the names I recalled, others I remembered, but couldn't put faces to. I asked her what it was all about and it was then that she explained all about FriendsReunited, something I had never heard of, especially as I had only just finished a beginners' computer course at night school. I didn't know much about the Internet or how e-mail worked etc. But when Julie finished explaining, I knew I just had to learn more. I asked her to read out the names from 1955 as I had left a year earlier than most of my classmates. I recognised a lot more names and when she read out the name Michael Harris, I couldn't believe it.

Mike Harris had been my best friend and the one that I had the longest contact with after leaving school. I had joined the Merchant Navy and then, in 1956, the Royal Navy. This naturally took me away from home, but we always got together when I was home on leave. During my service in the Royal Navy I met my future wife. We got married but she came from the 'other side of the water' in Lewisham and it was there that we settled and began to raise our family. As often happens when people leave their roots, friends drift apart and eventually we moved even further afield to Northamptonshire. The last contact we had was in about 1963. I did try to find Mike some years later by calling at his and his parents' last known addresses, but they had moved too. I guessed it was the end of our friendship and we would probably never see each other again.

Well, as Julie had explained, here was an opportunity to make contact with him. I immediately got myself an Internet server and signed up with FriendsReunited. I couldn't wait to e-mail him and sent him a letter telling him how I had found him and how I was so much looking forward to hearing back from him. I asked him what he was doing, what family he had, where he was living and could we possibly meet up again.

When I got his letter back, I just couldn't believe what he told me. He was living in ... *San Mateo, California* ... about three miles away from Julie who had introduced me to FrendsReunited in the first place.

In March this year, after making contact with more friends from our years, a reunion was held in a pub close to our old school and Mike came over with his son David to attend. As you can imagine, there were lots of laughs, a few tears and our friendship has now been firmly cemented with a vow never to lose touch again.

Michael O'Brien, Yorkshire

It was French author Marcel Proust who invented the 'Proustian rush' — that instant memory blast you get from tasting a childhood foodstuff. It's little wonder that food forms the basic ingredient of so many vivid memories — the meat and potatoes, if you will. It's all a matter of taste.

Marmite

'Did your mum give you this? Do you a) love it, or b) Hate it? I lurve it ... yum yum yum! Hubby hates it. Hubby goes to pub to watch rugby, hubby comes home tanked up and falls asleep in bath, hubby forgets he's promised to take wife out, wife gets narky and smears a thin coating of Marmite on unconscious hubby's lips. Tee-hee ... And he really *really* hates it.'

'Toast a slice of bread one side then cover the plain side with Marmite. Next slice garlic and onion on top then cover with cheese and toast until golden '

'Marmite and banana butties ... mmmmm ...'

'I remember going to a party once where a boy insisted on eating nothing but Marmite sandwiches, my friend's mum had to nip up the corner shop to get some! Funny how these obscure events stick in the mind!'

'Don't they build roads with it??'

'There was a craze of Marmite bashing a few years ago. Get a dollop of Marmite, on a plate, bash it quickly for a long time with a fork and it will turn a creamy white colour. Still tastes the same, though. Great for playing tricks on people who hate the stuff — they think they're eating margarine on their toast!'

'I saw a picture of Elton John having breakfast on his terrace in Nice, little silver tea trolley at his side with coffee etc. Peeking out behind the silver... a jar of Marmite. So he can't be all bad.'

Sugar Sandwiches and Crisp Sandwiches

'Anyone tried these in their youth? How about crisp sandwiches then?
Or am/was I strange?'

'Sugar sarnies were my faves, but I had to make them when my mum
wasn't around 'cos she thought they were disgusting and bad for me. Can't
have been that bad – still got all me teeth.'

'Plain crisps on bread with butter and Heinz Salad Cream. Yum!!'

'I used to like ... OK, OK, I still do ... Smash potato and baked bean
sandwiches.'

Unusual Combinations

'I used to eat lettuce dipped in sugar. I also loved condensed milk sandwiches.'

'Dry Weetabix with butter on.'

'I knew a girl from the Netherlands who loved to butter two slices of bread
then sprinkle a thick layer of hundreds and thousands between the slices
and tuck in. I thought she was odd.'

'I also used to put sugar in crunchy peanut butter sandwiches to make them
even crunchier!'

'I remember my nephew at the age of four going on a school trip and
having to take a packed lunch. He was totally devastated, 'cos he wanted to
take bread and dripping – or as he calls them "mucky fat butties", and my
sister told him that he wasn't going to shame her by taking dripping
butties ... On his return, he was most upset as two of his friends had taken
"mucky fat butties" to school, as well. So now she has had to give in
gracefully and accept that her now eight-year-old son just adores them.'

'My sister hated pilchards and the only way my mum could get her to eat
them was if she had them in a sandwich with jam!'

'I knew a bloke who was so tight he wouldn't spend much money on food, he would make things from whatever he got from the back of his cupboard, where most of it was out of date. One of his classics was a stale bread roll with half a Dairy Milk in it!'

'I know this sounds vile, but one of my favourite sandwiches has to be when you put strawberry jam on one slice of bread and Marmite on the other, then squish the two together. It's like a sweet-and-sour sandwich.'

'I remember a fad at school for toothpaste butties.'

'I like my Cup-A-Soups. I pulverise whatever flavour crisps are to hand, then add them, thus making a substantial meal.'

'A Fry's Chocolate Cream sliced very, very thinly, then put between two slices of slightly buttered bread. My dad was worse: he also liked to put orange segments on his. Now that is weird.'

School Dinners

Typical of the parallel universe that is the message boards was a long, drawn-out, cliffhanging saga about Gypsy Tart. One FriendsReunited member wanted to bake one exactly like she remembered from the school dinner hall. It's not in Delia, by the way. Thus, the resulting debate ran and ran, with updates from the cook herself. Rather than reproduce the whole sticky discussion, here's a flavour. (Sorry.)

'I have been following your trials and tribulations over the Gypsy Tart with bated breath over the last few days – even though I don't know what it is. We never had it in my day. I'm a little bit confused though that you are talking about evaporated milk and Gerard is talking about condensed milk. Two very different things. Could this be where the trouble is? Condensed milk is sticky and thick, evaporated milk is very runny.'

'To this day I can't eat semolina, or rice pudding.'

'I really loved my school meals, except for the mixed vegetables, they tasted like cardboard. My favourite pudding was what they called Swedish Apricot, which had mushy apricots at the bottom, cream in the middle and syrupy cornflakes at the top. The teachers claimed it as a dieter's nightmare.'

'I'll never forget semolina and prunes. One dollop of semolina and four prunes each. Nobody liked them on my table, so I used to eat 32 prunes. I still don't know anyone else who likes them!'

'Thank goodness for school dinners and the strict teachers who made us eat them, as well as enforcing proper table manners. I think today's kids are too fussy. I soon learnt the knack of getting the most food on my plate was to always stick up my hand when the teacher asked, "Who likes the burnt bits?" Today, I can eat and enjoy most anything, I've even tried fried mealworms, which I don't recommend – like eating cold, overbuttered popcorn – though live black ants are like acid-drops, quite tasty. The secret is to bite them before they bite you.'

'I just remembered the custard. Whoever was head of table for the day always used to ask "One lump or two?" I don't know which was worse, that or the tapioca pudding or maybe... the grey, mashed (lumpy) potato that you physically couldn't swallow, so you sat there with it in your mouth. You sat there with it an awful long time, as the teachers used to inspect you to make sure you'd swallowed every last bit before they'd let you leave the hall. This practice was abruptly brought to a halt when I threw up over one of them. Oh happy days!'

'Shortbread – so hard that when you tried to cut it half ended up on the floor and the other half shot down the table into the lap of the boy you had a crush on, or the meanest teacher in the school. If you were lucky, it wasn't covered in custard.'

'The dinner ladies were always as revolting as the meals they cooked weren't they? Usually grossly overweight with hairy chins. We used to think they ate all the good food and left us with the horrible stuff.'

Sweets

'Why is it all these great sweets have disappeared from the shelves? And what about Wagon Wheels – they're more like Dinky Car wheels now – not like the great big things that used to take me a quarter of an hour to eat at lunch break!'

'None of the sweets that you get now taste like they used to. Also they are a lot smaller. Do you think it's because we are bigger and our taste buds have altered?'

'Space Dust was the best, dead funny when you gave it to the dog.'

'I remember Ice Breaker, a mint cracknel, chocolate bar, which used to cut the roof of your mouth to shreds, it was so sharp. I think it was banned.'

'Our mum would give us money for collection at church on Sundays and we would go to the shop and buy Flying Saucers and Drumstick lollies.'

'Rainbow sherberts – you could tell all the girls who'd been eating it in break time by our multicoloured fingers where we'd dipped them in the bag.'

'I remember Spanish Gold. It was my fave of all the sweets. Looked like tobacco and tasted yummy. My mum used to send me to the bagwash with the week's washing, and I used to put the hot wash in with the warm so I could go the sweet shop next door for my Spanish Gold. It all came to an end when, by mistake, I put the warm wash in with the hot and my dad's jumpers came out about 12 inches short.'

'Does anyone remember strawberry and cream Blobs?'

'I remember eating too much sherbert, and then instantly vomiting it back down my nose.'

'I remember eating lots of Rice Paper. Did anyone else eat this? I also liked the sweets that looked like a cigarette. It even had red on one end

as if lit. Mum always told me that sweets were bad for me so I started smoking instead!'

'Have I got bigger or have Creme Eggs got smaller?'

'My husband spent one school summer working on the Curly Wurly machine at the Bourneville factory. My favourite story out of there was the time someone made the filling for the choccy eggs wrong and a whole batch of eggs in storage exploded!'

'As a child, I once bought a bar of Jamaican rum chocolate and remember buying a Curly Wurly along with it ... just in case they got suspicious and realised it WAS for me! I thought it was illegal to buy it under 18.'

Tears Are Not Enough

'Into each life some rain must fall,' wrote the American poet and scholar Henry Wadsworth Longfellow. It's worth remembering. The logo of HappyGroup, as seen at the bottom of every page on FriendsReunited and on their business cards too, is a beaming blue and yellow cat. It's apt. FriendsReunited is a happy place: it's about finding friends, fixing families, or simply having a laugh about school custard. But it can't be all smiles – life isn't like that. The search for an old acquaintance can lead to disappointment, even grief and pain. Either they passed away, or they're not as you remember them; the spark is gone. Worse, rekindling a relationship with someone from the past can damage a relationship from the present – though it's worth bearing in mind that, counter to the sensational coverage such tales receive in the papers, marriage break-ups form only a very tiny percentage of the tales told to us. These are not sob stories, simply ones that will move you, or make you reflect. Longfellow also wrote, 'Be still, sad heart, and cease repining; behind the clouds the sun is shining.'

All's Well That Ends

FriendsReunited caused the break up of my 24-year marriage. My ex-wife's lover's marriage had broken up the year before and he found her on FriendsReunited's workplaces section. They used to work together at RAF Holton in Buckinghamshire as nurses. He was her first real romance and I believe that had he not contacted her on FriendsReunited, I would still be married to her. I was happy in the marriage and loved her. I expect that this is pure Mills and Boon menopause on her part, trying to rekindle some lost love of years ago

She left me on the strength of just two dirty weekends with him and moved 318 miles away from her home, children, family and friends in Southampton, to live in Holyhead, Anglesey.

I had no idea that she had been having this affair. We had been on holiday on the Italian Riviera just two weeks before she left. I thought that the holiday had been just fine. She gave no hint during that fortnight that she was unhappy with our marriage. She was supposed to be on a three-day business seminar in the days preceding her leaving. And because it was held where she used to live and work before we were married, she asked if she could also stay the weekend there and look up old friends and visit old haunts. When she arrived home at 7.00 p.m. on the Sunday, she just came right out with it, told me about the affair and said that she was leaving me right away to be with him.

The children and her parents all took it very badly: son (22) got drunk that night and lost his driving licence; daughter (21) left her university degree course half way through suffering from clinical depression. Her relationship with her parents will never be the same. I am probably closer to them now than they are to their own daughter.

Initially, I was very upset and wrote a stinkingly sarcastic letter to FriendsReunited thanking them for their part in ruining our marriage, but things have changed since then.

I am enjoying my freedom immensely, going out jiving three or four times a week, which has meant that I am lighter, fitter and more energetic than I have been for years.

My circle of friends is much larger and I am dating girls up to ten years younger than my former wife and usually they are prettier and more vivacious too.

This all happened early last July and I got my divorce the Wednesday after Easter. I have bought my wife out of the house and continue to run my own advertising business, so I can maintain the same standard of living.

The divorce has been amicable. I do not consider that we are friends any longer; friends do not cheat and lie on each other. But we are civil to each other. When the divorce came through, we actually opened a bottle of champagne and toasted each other's future happiness!

So, perhaps the time has come to actually thank FriendsReunited for making all this possible! I am sure that what I will end up with will be better than what I had.

Peter Rea, Southampton

The Grandfather Clock

When I was in Bermondsey Central School during the fifties, each year two prizes were awarded for the best true story written by the pupils.

There was a boy in our class, Stephen, who used to get picked on for having holey trousers, or a grubby shirt, and it was his story that I have remembered all these years on, which was read out in class as he had won a prize.

His family had a grandfather clock in their house which always kept perfect time. One day it stopped, at exactly the time his father died, never to work again — even though his mother had clockmakers come to look at it, they could find nothing wrong.

This caused quite a stir in our class — Stephen had never told anyone that his father had died. His poor mum had to bring the children up on her own, which was harder in those days as money from the DSS was not as forthcoming as it is now. From that day on Stephen was treated with love and respect, but the memory of that day will stay with me forever.

Christine Anderson (née Hill), Cuxton, Kent

These Are The Breaks

This is an unhappy love story.

Just before I left school, aged 16, I met and fell deeply in love with a young lady from the same school. We went out together for six months before I joined the navy. We said we would write to each other and continue to see each other whenever I was on leave. Unfortunately a letter I wrote to her was read by her father and he forbade us to see each other again. Although we did meet once or twice, she was reluctant to go against her father's wishes and we lost contact. Whilst I was serving overseas I met a mutual friend of ours and was told that she had got married and was expecting a child.

I was heartbroken, but have remained in love with her and think of her often, even now after thirty years.

In January this year, I received an e-mail through FriendsReunited from a person whom I do not know with a message from the girl I knew. I was thrilled and sent a reply asking her to contact me again, but alas after four months I have not heard from her again.

Bruce Bayliss, Somerset

Life Sometimes Isn't Fair

I suppose this story is just about hang-ups. Schoolchildren can often carry a lot more baggage than the usual text books.

Coming from a motherless family, with my father out of work and taking care of the home, we were poor. The shame and insecurities that attached themselves to this fact grew as did I. We all hear the stories, how poor this or that person was as a child. But I tell you being poor in the late seventies was probably a lot harder. They were the days when Mr Average had a car, a telephone, and took holidays, and his children had pocket money, bicycles and Easter eggs at Easter. Even our working-class neighbours appeared to have more. Gone were the days when everyone had nothing; now it was only the Lovells. I suppose at the time I was too young and embarrassed to thank the few people that saw past my 'Stig of the Dump' exterior and showed me kindness.

I never went on school trips at St Edmunds, Wolverhampton. I was always the one to stay behind, sitting in lessons with the class below, whilst the rest of my classmates went off for the day with their packed lunches and spending money to some exotic location. I think I spent the majority of my childhood being jealous of everyone that wasn't me. Alton Towers was the place, I think £1 was the cost. Not much?

Lisa Candal, whom I considered to be the most beautiful girl in the school – always seemed to be centre of the universe, very popular, intelligent and, of course, pretty – knew I wasn't going. So she paid for me to go. I had a great time: once inside, all the rides were free, so I didn't need any spending money and for once I was with the rest of the class. I couldn't remember thanking her, although I probably did. For this action boosted the little confidence I had and made me see that it wasn't, as my father put it, 'them and us'.

I joined FriendReunited for the sole purpose of thanking her. She now lives in Australia with her three children and I in Switzerland. Upon receiving e-mails, she told me that at the time her parents were getting a divorce, so money was really tight for her family, and she had to work the weekends at the Birmingham Rag Market help out. At least now I was able to thank her properly and let her know how much that action helped me and how I never forgot her and what she did.

One more thing regarding human nature: a caring person such as Lisa continues to work in a caring profession – she works in a cardiothoracic intensive care unit.

Paul Lovell, Switzerland

Stairway To Heaven

There were three children in our family, Ingrid (myself), Margaret and Leslie
Weller. As children we were very close to each other and were always
together. Born in the mid to late forties we grew up in Kent in a world where
children could go out to play and wander around without fear of coming to
harm. We all went to the same schools in Welling and were very happy and
content.

Growing up as a trio was great – we rarely fell out. I was the eldest,
Leslie the youngest and there were only three years between us. As the
youngest and the only boy he was spoilt. If we played board games and he
was losing, he would toss the whole board up in the air. He never got into
trouble for doing it and it did cause some slight resentment, but we loved
him so it was no big deal. He was very protected and in some ways, when in
later life, just before his death, things went wrong, he could not handle
them very well.

He had two great passions, music and football. He supported Arsenal all
his life. He used to take an old trumpet to their matches and took great
delight in blowing it loudly whenever they scored.

But music was his greatest love. I can still remember the sound of very
loud records emanating from our front room and my dad yelling out to turn
it down! As was the fashion in the sixties, he grew his hair very long and
wore very scruffy clothes, much to the distress of my parents. Just as they
thought his appearance could not get any worse, he bought a ladies' fur coat
for 50p at a jumble sale and proceeded to wear it whenever possible, even in
the summer. He had loads of friends and they were always out and about.
With his great height he could not be missed and, it has to be said, he did get
some very strange looks.

When he was 21 he contracted diabetes and from then on he had to rely on
insulin injections. He found it hard to adjust because he played guitar with
his group and, because he had to have regular balanced meals, it was
difficult to travel around with the rest of the group, so he had to give it up.

Eventually he did adjust and in 1973 moved to Jersey with his parents and
grandmother. Nine months later, he married and was very happy for a
number of years. As can happen, fate decided his life had been too good and
that it was time to throw in some nasties. In a very short space of time he

had a car accident, his wife left him and he broke an ankle playing football. His stress caused him to lose his appetite which made balancing his insulin with the correct amount of food very difficult.

In April 1979, our mother, worried because he had not arrived for lunch with her, went to his flat and discovered that he had died. He was 30 years old. The shock and grief for us all was almost unbearable. Our father, who was suffering with cancer, deteriorated rapidly and died in July the following year, aged 59. At 2.30 a.m., on the morning of his funeral, our grandmother died. Margaret and I brought our much loved mum back to Hampshire. Although she settled into a happy life with us, losing her son, husband and mother in such a short space of time inevitably left its mark and she died in 1988. She was only 65 years old.

Margaret and I still live in Hampshire. Our way of dealing with life is to laugh a lot when something goes wrong.

The last time I saw Leslie was on one of my visits to Jersey to see the family. He looked great and had just settled into the flat where three months later he would die. We talked about him coming to visit my husband and me. Shortly after that his world crashed about him and he was too depressed to do anything. I wish with all my heart I could put the clock back to a week before he died. I would fly out to Jersey, take him home, talk through his problems and get him to eat.

Leslie was always an extremely popular person who made friends wherever he went. He was a handsome 6' 6" gentle giant with a wicked sense of humour. If there is a heaven, we are sure he is there, maybe strumming a guitar and talking to his idol Jimi Hendrix. We miss him.

Ingrid Weller-Wrench, Tadley, Hampshire

That Was Glen

Some 24 years ago, my parents took me out of the state secondary school I was in and dumped me in a dreadful private school. At the secondary school, I used to sit next to a boy called Glen Smart, as they insisted we sat boy/girl. We were only around 13 when I left. I didn't really know Glen until they sat him next to me, but looked around at the other boys who either were perching as far away as they could from the 'girl germs' or making lecherous comments (depending on the advancement of their hormones, I suppose). I was very lucky; Glen was great fun to sit with, helped me in dreadful science, and chatted and giggled – we had great fun.

Shortly after I left the school, Glen was on his bike and was killed in a hit-and-run accident – they never found the driver.

Glen had an older brother, whom I never knew, called Gary. I found him on FriendsReunited a year or so ago and contacted him to let him know that Glen had not been forgotten. Far from it. I had named my second son after him but added an extra 'n' for fear of history repeating itself.

I am now in regular contact with Gary, and had a very touching letter from Gary and Glen's mother.

Sadly, the likelihood is that now I am living in Perth, in Australia, we will not be able to meet up. The weird thing is though, that both Glen(n)s have a face full of freckles – no one in my family has a face full of freckles – and I wonder if they would be there if I had named him Dave or John.

Sarah Mahoney, Perth, Australia

You Keep Me Hanging On

I am a naturally nosey(!) and helpful person, and I like to do a good turn if possible. I read on the notice board that someone from my school was desperately trying to get in touch with an old school friend without much luck, so I looked into my own records and found two people with the surname that he was looking for. I duly reported back to him (Gary) and left it there, not expecting for one minute to get any response.

I had an e-mail to say he had tried the addresses once and had almost given up when his wife said try again, so he did and, lo and behold, he found his friend from 20-odd years past. He e-mailed me and was quite delighted that I had helped him and couldn't express his thanks enough. I was very touched indeed. I was Gary's 'new best friend' he said.

Then, after having a few more thank yous from him and his wife, I received an e-mail to say Gary had passed away; he had been suffering from cancer for many years and had hung on long enough to find his pal, which his wife and he said was all thanks to me. To say I was gutted was an understatement, I was so very pleased that I had helped him.

I sent condolences to his family and received some really touching poems and writings back from them and a delightful Easter card. I felt very humble, but also bursting with pride, that they should take the trouble to be so kind.

It really is true that if you are kind it comes back a hundred fold. I am proud to have known you Gary, even if it was only by e-mail, and I know you are watching over your lovely family.

Anon

This Isn't The End

I split up with my ex-partner after he found his first love on the website. I was eight-and-a-half months pregnant when he started an affair with her and, only four weeks after our son was born, he announced that our relationship was over. I was devastated, but now I am living on my own with my son in our own house and I have returned to full-time work and have just completed my HNC in Computing, so I am really proud of myself and
my son.

Alicia Black, Dudley Port, West Midlands

My Friend Sarah

At the age of five, when I started school, I found a 'best friend' with whom I shared a lifetime of memories over the next 11 years, until we left school. We were drawn to each other because from the outset we were both very shy and found difficulty mixing easily with the other girls. If the class had to pair off, we were always together, walking in the famous (or infamous) crocodile line and, as the years went on and we were growing up, we shared out worries, happiness, feelings and experiences.

Sarah was a beautiful girl with long, curly, black hair framing a pretty little face, whereas I was very plain with short, straight hair and as we grew older she became even prettier and I often wondered why she should stick with me and because of that I adored her. I excelled at gymnastics and sports while Sarah was good at lessons and often helped me what I got stuck.

When we were about 15, her parents asked me if I would like to stay with them for a while and I couldn't resist seeing how Sarah and her family lived. She was an only child and her parents were lovely people. They lived in the country and introduced me to the delights of fields, woods and mountain etc, a world I had never been in before. The time went too quickly and then it was back to start studying for O-levels.

Sarah did well in the examinations and I didn't do so badly either and soon after that we parted. I went on to become a medical secretary and, although we wrote to each other for a while, Sarah suddenly stopped writing and I never heard from her again. But one of my other friends had an idea that she had become pregnant while unmarried, which I found hard to believe.

I had been married for almost 40 years and had acquired a computer. One day, I came across FriendsReunited and thought here is my chance to trace Sarah. Through various means I eventually learnt what had happened to her.

I received an e-mail from a young lad asking if I had known his mother (he had found my name through FriendsReunited). Apparently, she had died having a baby and he knew very little about her and just wanted a little information as to what she had been like. He did not know his father.

To cut a long story short, it transpires that his mother had indeed been my 'best friend' and although I couldn't give him much information, I told him all I could about her – about her likes and dislikes, her pretty appearance and the good times we had together. I received one e-mail from him thanking me for giving him some insight into her character and that was the last that I heard.

A sad ending to my story, but even so it was an ending.

Joady Hodskinson

Liz, Lynn and Me

I only have the age old story I am afraid, but it means a lot to us.

Liz and I were best friends through grammar school – the 'poor' pair in the class really and we spent many hours together out of school too – in part hero worshipping first *The Man from U.N.C.L.E.* then The Monkees.

When I left school at 17, I ran away from home and thereby everyone else I knew.

Over the ensuing years, I tried several ways to track Liz down, but to no avail. Eventually, I was made aware of the FriendsReunited site and immediately joined with the sole intention of hopefully regaining contact with Liz.

We have now been 'reunited' for a year and a half and, luckily, live within half an hour's drive of each other, so meet up most months. She had had the same experiences in trying to contact me and we are both as pleased as punch to be back in touch and still very good friends.

Our getting together is made somewhat more poignant by the fact that the one school friend I had managed to keep in touch with – Lynn – who was part of our group of four at school, came with me to meet Liz last year just once before very sadly dying in January. Liz is not a replacement for this very valued friendship, but we are both very glad we have found each other. I'd better add that we are now 51, so it was one heck of a long gap.

Margaret Wilson

Of course, what parents used to say can be disarmingly similar to what we, as parents, say ourselves. Many a generation has uttered the words, 'I didn't think,' only to be hit with the evergreen, 'That's your trouble – you don't think!'

'When asked what I wanted for Christmas, I once said, "A bike." To which my dad replied, "I'll bike you in a minute"!'

'As soon as someone passed wind in the house, Dad would shout, "Come in vicar, wipe your feet!" No one knew who the real culprit was, but I have a sneaky suspicion it was Dad who had "dropped one".'

'If she had eaten rather too much, like at Christmas for example, my gran used to complain of having a "belly like a poisoned pup". Frighteningly, I find myself using the phrase too!'

'When my friend would catch his son picking his nose, he'd say, "When you get to the bridge, give us a wave".'

'My mum used to say, if someone fancied you, that they were "hanging their hat up to you".'

'You're as helpful as a one-legged person at a bum-kicking contest.'

'"Eat your crusts, it'll make your hair curly". Like the pinnacle to all your mother's hopes and aspirations was to have a kid with curly hair.'

'You look like you've been dragged through a hedge backwards.'

'Don't sit with your back to the fire, else your backbone will melt. It's looking gloomy over by Bill's mother's (who the hell is Bill?).'

'Anyone dashing around in a disorganised manner was known to be "flying around like a fart in a colander". Mother, really!'

'We lived with my grandparents, and my gran had lots of sayings. When we misbehaved, she would say, "I'll smack your bum with a tea leaf until it bleeds!"'

If I asked my mum what was for dinner, she would say, "Shim Shams for blind horses" – never did like the taste!'

'My mum would say, "Fried bread with spit on it". We were so grateful when it wasn't!'

'When I asked the same question, my mum would say: "Air Pie without the crust".'

'Or, "Three kicks at the pantry door".'

'Bread and Pullit followed by Windmill Pie.'

'Eat your carrots; they're good for your eyes. You don't see rabbits wearing glasses.'

'If you pull a face and the wind changes, it'll stick like that.'

'If you swallow that chewing gum, you will have chewing gum trees growing inside your stomach.'

'If you complained that food was hot in our house, you would always get: "So would you be, if you had been in the oven on gas mark 5 for 40 minutes". Another favourite: if you asked if you could leave the table, the reply would always be "Well you can't take it with you".'

'"This is going to hurt me more than it hurts you" – said just before you got a hiding. Yeah, right Dad.'

'You'll be laughing on the other side of your face in a minute!'

'From my grandmother: "Looking like the wreck of the Hesperus" – about an untidy or scruffy person.'

'"Woe betide you, if I find out you're lying…" For years I thought the actual word was "woby-tied" and I was too scared to ask what it meant!'

All You Need Is Love

Love is . . . a spirit all compact of fire. Love is . . . the wisdom of the fool and the folly of the wise. Love is . . . like oxygen, you get too much you get too high, not enough and you're gonna die. (William Shakespeare, Samuel Johnson, The Sweet.) Love is . . . a subject that has exercised our greatest minds. Not surprisingly, it forms the mother lode of many of the best stories we received. Not all old flames can, or should, be fanned, and not all of these stories end with a diamond on the finger, but all speak of the awkwardness and elation of romance. The standard text used to be 'boy meets girl'. Now we must add, 'boy meets girl again after 18 years thanks to FriendsReunited, falls in love all over again and ends up marrying girl.' For the record, the first FriendsReunited marriage is said to be that of Matt Bascombe and Rae-Sarah Weedon ('We have never been so happy and contented with life,' says Matt). The first FriendsReunited baby — after what can only be called a race for the prize between three couples! — was born in September 2002: Dylan Livingstone, son of Annette and Simon Smythe. Dylan weighed in at 8lb 10oz.

I Can't Live If Living Is Without You

Back in the early 1970s I attended Lister Technical School in Plaistow, East London. One evening, I went to one of the school socials, which was basically a disco, and being shy, I didn't have the courage to ask any of the girls to dance. However, near the end of the evening, a girl asked me if I wanted to ask her friend to dance, which I did. We danced to 'Without You' by Nilsson and I was in love! After a few weeks, the 'romance' fizzled out, but even through adulthood I never forgot my first love.

Cut to 2002, about 28 years later, and a friend tells me about FriendsReunited. As I went through the leavers of 1976 list I saw her name! I was hesitant about replying to her e mail address, but I did anyway. Her notes said she was now divorced, as I am (I'm 44 and she is 43). She replied to my e-mail, then we exchanged phone numbers, and a few months on, in August 2002, we met for the first time in nearly 30 years.

We met at Euston Station, as she was living in the Midlands and I in Essex, and since that day she has transformed my life. We are in love and plan to marry sometime this year!

I have given a lot of thought as to why I have such a strong connection with Kathy after this length of time. I believe it is because during your teenage years you are particularly impressionable to outside influences and, as Kathy was my first love, she seems somehow to have been imprinted on me psychologically. Perhaps my personality is particularly susceptible, because I'm also fixated with the music of that era — the early seventies. Having talked to other people about this many have said they too have a special person from their past that they would love to see again, so maybe I'm not that different!

As for the art of getting back together, in our case we have both been through difficult past relationships, so when we met again without any ties we found that we were both sympathetic towards each other and it formed a good basis for a relationship.

During the first two months we would talk for up to five hours on the phone and a lot of the conversations related to shared experiences as teenagers, like Glam Rock, sweets, clothes and places in the East End of London. I also know that luck has played a big part, because we met at a time when we were both in a position to embark on a new relationship and we probably both needed someone. I must say though, that Kathy did question whether I was in love with the nostalgia of our past and not the real adult woman of today! (I have told her that it is a combination of the two.)

On 22 August 2003, Kathy and I were married at Norwich Register Office, almost a year to the day of our meeting each other again. I am of course very grateful for FriendsReunited as I have fallen in love with and married that special person from my past.

David Chivers, Romford, Essex

Divine Intervention

I suppose I'd always been a shy, insecure kind of child, but as I got to the end of my school days I'd gained a lot of confidence, even becoming form captain at one point. As soon as I was 18, I started training to be a nurse and almost at the same time left my first lover, John (the boy next door) and became infatuated with a bastard (excuse me!) who treated me badly and soon dumped me. With self-esteem at rock bottom and plagued by insecurity, I set about having a good time, and managed quite a good job of it. Except that underneath I was still terrified and insecure. Pretty soon I met the man who became my husband, and marriage quickly followed.

I gave up my training and within a year we had our first baby. But I was still afraid, worried about being abandoned – God knows why – my husband never gave me the slightest reason to worry about that. So I started going to church because life seemed kind of empty and I was feeling guilty for being a backsliding Christian. I went to the local Methodist church and soon my husband started going too. I think the strict Christian rules about marriage made me feel safer. But soon I got disillusioned with the Methodists, and when I heard of this super-strict church, I was deeply impressed. So we left everything and moved to the West Country to join them.

There isn't time to go into detail about this church, except to say it was extremely strict: no drinking, smoking, TV, radio, contraception, makeup, magazines, or cinema etc. You didn't have much contact with anyone outside the church, especially if you were a mother at home. Women were not allowed to wear trousers, men had to have very short hair.

Those were the sort of rules. But nobody ever said they were rules. Officially, everybody was free to do what they liked, but we all knew they were rules and if we didn't stick to them, we would never really be accepted. Most people believed they were right anyway, God's will for us, intended to make us happy. They were very keen on maintaining 'God's order' for men and women – basically men and women are not equal in the eyes of God. Women were created to help and serve men, and are 'the weaker vessel'. Men were intended to have authority, women to submit. That sounds like my dad's philosophy, and maybe that was a factor in why I subconsciously thought it must be right, even though I didn't like it.

Looking back now, I find it hard to believe I went along with so many doctrines that went directly against my personal feelings. It was a bit like being buried alive in a way. There's a whole chunk of time – from about the late seventies to the mid nineties – that I missed. I missed the eighties almost completely. I knew about the Falklands war, and I knew who the Prime Minister was, but that was about it. I couldn't tell you anything about the music, fashion, politics, or world events of any kind really. Current affairs went completely unnoticed, and now it's just a big gap in my social memory.

More disturbing than the outward restrictions and rules was the mind control exercised by the church. I don't think they see it as that, but that's what it amounts to. I think there's a desire in many people to have power over others in one way or another. A need to control or manipulate, and religion can be a very good tool for this. If you can tap into someone's need for God and convince them you are his spokesperson, you can get them to do almost anything if their need is strong enough.

Of course, things did happen to me through all those 'blank' years. They were very full and busy ones, as I was almost always pregnant, or had a child under two (I have ten children). And I do have some good memories of those days, but mostly I remember the tiredness and hard work of raising all those children. They brought me a lot of joy too; they still do.

My social life was centred completely on the church, and it was busy. We often had visitors and when the many conferences and special conventions were on, there would be entire families with lots of kids to stay. Couples would get together for evenings of fellowship, but it would be difficult to connect on any other level. I don't remember many people in the church whom I really felt I could be friends with on a human level in the ordinary way. It wasn't encouraged to have special friends anyway.

Things began to change in the nineties after a new leader took over. He was a younger man who could see that the church couldn't survive without change. There was a huge revival, which had a big effect on all of us. People went kind of crazy with zeal, the meetings livened up considerably. It was like mass hysteria, and I wasn't sure I trusted all that extreme fervour. With the big increase in zeal came also increased personal freedom in outward things. For example, people began to watch videos, listen to the radio, or go to see a film occasionally. Girls began to wear trousers, if they had a valid reason like a hiking trip or something.

There were meetings all the time and fellowship would often continue late into the night.

But the mind control tightened up even more in a way. There were what I thought of as witch hunts. If spiritual development was not going as quickly as certain people thought it should, then they would start asking why. Whose fault is it? Who is not in the right spirit? They would decide who was holding back the spiritual development of the church and in effect put them out of the fellowship.

After a while this happened to me, and it was the worst experience of my life. It felt like my whole world had fallen down round my ears. I couldn't understand what I'd done wrong. I was so used to thinking the church was always right that it was hard to question why this was happening. It wasn't anything official of course, just an understanding among 'the Congregation' that I was in some sort of spiritual disgrace. To cope with this, I tried to believe they were right and not to believe what I suspected was really the truth, whch was that I had offended a certain lady, who had worked her way by sheer zeal and force of personality to a position of unofficial power in the local church and beyond. The worst thing in all this was that my sister also turned her back on me. She'd speak to me and wasn't openly nasty, but the warm, close, friendly relationship we'd had since we were children just stopped. She'd always been my best friend, and I just fell apart inside when this happened.

In a way it was a good thing, because it made me realise that the church had this power to control what people thought and believed, and didn't have the spiritual insight to see and put a stop to what was going on.

Eventually, my sister was given the cold shoulder too, and was as devastated as I'd been. But we made it up with each other and led a rebellion to stop this awful woman doing any more harm. It was becoming obvious to many folk that far from the church developing in a good way, numbers in the inner circle were dwindling. She decided to move away and things settled back down. But I don't think they were ever really the same again.

Years went by. I began to question more things in my own mind and became less willing to submit to the dictates of the church and also to the will of my husband, but I still didn't want to let go of the church. I was beginning to realise that I preferred it when my husband was away, and he often was. When he wasn't working, he was busy in the church. He would often go away to conferences and meetings. Many times I saw in the New Year alone, or Easter and even our wedding anniversary in July. If any family birthday fell on a meeting day, it was too bad. In short, the church came first, then the business, then the children and me. It was 20 years before we even went out for a day together without the children.

Then we had a week together in Morocco in March 2000 and by this time I was, frankly, bored with his company. He didn't seem all that interested in what I wanted to talk about. He had his opinions and didn't see any need to revise them. He didn't like those opinions challenged, or to be disagreed with.

I was frustrated being at home, clearing up after everybody day after day, week after week, year after year, with no end to it in sight. When we moved out of town to a lovely house, I thought I was going to be happy. We chose it for the benefit of the church really, as they didn't have a meeting place of their own and there was plenty of room here. We took on a huge mortgage to be able to buy it, and the church certainly did make use of it. Soon, everything seemed to happen at our place — Bonfire Night, family days, celebrations of all kinds, young people's meetings, children's meetings and all sorts of things. There was a lot of catering and hospitality involved, so a lot of extra work. After a hectic two years, the church bought a meeting place and we were no longer needed. Well, I wasn't really. My husband Dave was, as there was a lot of work to do on the new meeting hall and he's a very practical man. He worked himself into the ground helping to get the place into shape.

I was becoming increasingly worried about the way the church was always asking for money. It never used to be like that, but more and more things were geared towards getting more money out of the church members and urging them to work harder.

In September 2001, I got in touch with John (my 'childhood sweetheart') again. I saw his name on the FriendsReunited website and in his notes it said, 'Rose, please get in touch,' so I did. I sent him a brief e-mail outlining where I was now and what I was doing, and he answered the next day.

Almost from the first e-mail there was something there between us, a kind of spark. Soon we were writing to each other daily, very platonic and all that, but no way was I going to stop, even though Dave said I had to. I felt I was waking from a long sleep.

John spoke to the Rose he used to know, to the real, essential me under all those layers of brainwashing and self-delusion. He spoke to me as a person in my own right, as someone who was an individual, as his equal. Here was someone who seemed to know me, to be interested in what I had to say.

I found him even more interesting than he was as a youth. We 'talked' about all kinds of things, from the trivial to the deeply spiritual. I started to open my mind even more to reason and became more confident to challenge the church's hold on my mind and intellect. He gave me confidence to trust my own judgement. In short, I was beginning to realise I had found a kindred spirit and I knew he was feeling the same.

It wasn't too many months before we both realised we'd fallen in love again, although we didn't say so as yet. We decided to meet, and from that point on we knew it was real and it wasn't going to go away. That was a year ago, and we spent lots of time together even though we lived 70 miles apart.

I left the church officially in June last year, although I'd decided it wasn't for me any more months earlier. Dave was very upset, but vowed it wouldn't make any difference to his commitment. My sister was devastated and couldn't understand why I hadn't confided in her.

Dave found out about John in September. He was extremely angry and hurt, but I told him I couldn't give him up. The last thing I wanted to do was to hurt anyone, but I couldn't face the thought of life without John, of going back to how things were, of spending the rest of my life with a dominating man I didn't love any more.

I'd wanted to reach out to life beyond the kitchen sink before it was too late, to achieve something, to be my own person. Dave had said I could go to college as long as I could get all the housework done as well (impossible!). That hurt me so much.

I took a voluntary job in a charity shop to get me out into the real world. Going to college to do a personal development course did me a lot of good, and also helped me gain confidence. It also helped me to find out more about myself, and to talk about myself (very difficult after years of being taught not to) and to be honest about my feelings – to be able to say 'I'm angry', for instance, without feeling instantly condemned as a sinner.

And so up to the present day.

Dave and I have separated, which I can't feel regret over, except that the children have been through a hard time. I'm buying a house with John, and the three youngest children live with us, and the two grown up older ones who haven't left home yet live with Dave.

I want to live a 'normal' life, whatever that is. I want to finish the sociology A-level I'm taking and do well in it. I'm enjoying intellectual freedom, still exploring ideas and ways of looking at things. What I do regret is that I've lost the close friendship I had with my sister.

My love for John keeps growing, and the more time I spend with him the more I want to be with him always. I sometimes wonder why I don't feel guilty after all the years of strictness. But I don't, and my ideas about God and life are still under revision!

Now, at the age of 45, my life is full of promise for the future and whatever it holds, I'm looking forward to it.

Rose Lawrence, West Country

Swingers

I remember back in 1974 taking my new girlfriend to a friend's party, where lo and behold I was the only bloke to have a girl in tow. To my horror, after having a few drinks and totally ignoring my date, I found her in bed with not one, but half a dozen of my so-called friends. Needless to say, they weren't sleeping. Still I suppose that's part of growing up.

Roy Harrocks, Lancing, West Sussex

Love Like Diamond

I logged on to FriendsReunited to be confronted with names that I hadn't heard for 26 years. Old memories came flooding back and some names were more familiar than others. Some names were very unfamiliar; surely I hadn't gone through five years of education with some of these people.

One name stood out to me. I had vague memories of sitting in a field at the age of 12 discussing the various pros and cons of baths versus showers with this particular boy. Curiosity got the better of me, I decided to e-mail this 'boy' and see what had become of him. I soon got a reply and regular e-mails were then exchanged, some factual (catching up on family events over the last 26 years), some funny and some flirty. We arranged to meet one Saturday night with a group of school friends. To cut a very long story very short, I am typing this with a diamond on my finger and soon will exchange wedding vows with the now very grown-up boy. By the way... we prefer showers.

Linda Hamilton, Lincoln

Planes, Trains ...

I am now a 59-year-old teacher, shortly to be retired, divorced for 20 years with four grown-up children, one in Australia.

When I was 15 on a week's holiday at the seaside near Edinburgh, I met a boy of 19 who was mad about aeroplanes and worked in Prestwick. Later, he went to Manchester to work for another aeroplane company, but still came up on the old steam train to see me. We loved one another, although we never said the words, and I was too young for those days to get involved sexually.

At 18, I went to university and the sixties were in full swing, barriers had come down, and I was ready for a full relationship. On my first day at university I met someone else, got involved with him and eventually married at 20. I had of course written the usual exit letter to the other boy and received a cursory note in reply.

I knew I had made the wrong choice before I was married and tried to get my first boyfriend back, but he was too proud; he himself was now going out with someone else (whom he eventually married six years later without much enthusiasm)

I had a very turbulent marriage and often thought wistfully of the happiness I had had with my much regretted ex who, by now, had left the country to work with aeroplanes in Israel. Every few years I used to phone his mother without revealing my name to find out where in the world he was ... but in my thirties I gave up.

In October 2002, almost forty years to the date of our last meeting in 1964, he contacted me, finding me on the website and, after one letter, it was all on again, albeit long distance with daily e-mail letters, the odd short visit and twice weekly telephone calls.

There is no happy ending to this story, because he's too old to give up a whole life lived in America, which includes his own unfortunate marriage, but we are again very much in love with each other and will keep this relationship going until the end of time. He's still working with aeroplanes.

One of the bittersweet things about it all is that we met when we were too young to know that this first relationship for us both would turn out in the end to be the best one of our whole lives. I certainly never imagined that when we were laughing together as youngsters that neither of us would ever laugh like that again until we met 40 years later. What happened when that e-mail arrived last October was the most magical and wonderful moment of my whole life and contact with him has healed me of a lifetime's wounds. He could never have found me again in any other way. I owe FriendsReunited my past, present and future feelings for the only man I have ever really loved.

Anonymous

Oh Well

I joined FriendsReunited and got an e-mail from Martyn Kay, my first
boyfriend! He is now an airline pilot. We were at Penistone Grammar School,
near Barnsley, and left in 1980 ... but there's been no re-kindling of the
romance, I'm afraid, as I'm now married.

Joanne Penney (née Sykes), Stocksbridge, Sheffield

Band Of Gold

Our story began over 50 years ago!

Mel J was a very bright little boy at Peacock Street School, Manchester. He
was an only child, his mother unfortunately killed in the Manchester blitz, and
was cared for by several aunties and a fairly strict father. Joyce P was in the
same class as Mel, and lived around the corner from school with one younger
brother and a newly divorced, hard-working mother.

At the age of ten there was a lot of scholarly rivalry, lots of playing
together and a considerable amount of teasing going on. Mel would very
often be 'hanging around' Joyce's home after school, until one day he brought
something very special for Joyce. Imagine the delight when an engagement
ring was produced, an engagement between two ten year olds! Unfortunately
– and this was devastating to Joyce – the ring had to be returned when it
was discovered to be a genuine gold ring, in fact, Mel's late mother's
engagement ring.

The following year everything changed, as the two separated to go to
different grammar schools, and from Joyce's perspective that was the end of
the story and the last she would see of the cheeky little boy with the big
brown eyes. Not so for Mel, however. Unknown to his sweetheart, he had
visited her home once or twice to see her, but had had no luck in the contact.
The letters he had so carefully composed were never posted due to family
circumstances and, as things gradually deteriorated at home, he left school,
aged 15, and 'ran away to sea'.

The idea of being in touch with the girl with the long fair hair would not go
away, however, and on leave from the Fleet Air Arm, he tried one last time to

get in touch. He plucked up enough courage after five years to send a photo of himself in naval uniform, enclosing his address and asking if Joyce would like to write to him from time to time.

Joyce never received that photograph and was under the impression that Mel had disappeared from her life. During the following 50 years she often thought of the boy she was so briefly engaged to, but had no idea that Mel had been trying to contact her. Mel continued with his naval career thinking that his ex-fiancée wanted nothing more to do with him, since no letters were ever received.

Fifty years passed. Mel acquired a computer, Joyce discovered FriendsReunited and ... BINGO! Mel received only one contact from FriendsReunited, Joyce received only one contact from FriendsReunited. Guess who they were from!

Joyce Windsor, New Zealand

Girls And Boys
I came across the name of a certain 'boy' that I recognised on one of my first visits to FriendsReunited. I remembered that this was one of my first young romances — it probably lasted about four weeks, and I remember this 'boy' spending the whole length of a film trying to put his arm around me, with friends sitting behind us encouraging and giggling! We must have been about 14. Cannot remember details of our 'split' — who chucked who etc — but his details on the website now mention that he lives in Brighton with his partner... David! Was his early experience with me enough to put him off women for life? I have quite a complex nowadays! Have not dared to contact him and ask!

Sarah Flinton, Derby

Love Grows
I went to Harlington Secondary School in Middlesex, from 1969 to 1974. All through school we were in the same form group. I knew who he was and

apparently he knew me but that was, as they say, that. Until one day last year ...

I had been fiddling around with the computer and I received a message to say that a new member had joined for my year. I scrolled through the names and there it was: a blast from the past. I sent a message saying that yes, I remembered him and wondered if he remembered me. I gave a brief description of myself: red hair, hair band, glasses, freckles and goofy teeth. To my horror he replied and said he did remember me.

I wasn't too sure if it was my name that rang a bell or the graphic description of myself but I was amazed at other things he remembered about me. The fact that I was the only one by the fourth year still to be wearing long white socks and that I was a huge fan of Marc Bolan and T Rex. I was flattered. Even though I recall us scrapping in the corridor in first year.

After a number of e-mails between us he sent me his phone number and said that it might be good to chat. I put off phoning for a while, then one evening I plucked up the courage. That was over a year ago now and we haven't stopped chatting since. In fact, we have been seeing each other. I have been wined and dined and treated like a real lady. We went to Canada in April this year and then on a Mini Cruise for four days. He is a really wonderful man. I have really begun to enjoy my life again and I want to thank him from the bottom of my heart and tell my wonderful partner I love him very much. His name is Richard Millett.

Jeanette Dack

Lucky Break

One of my very first boyfriends that I knew during my late teens contacted me through FriendsReunited; we corresponded for about two months over the Internet and became very close and intimate over the period of Spring–Summer 2002. We had very long conversations every day – all on my mobile phone as I had to call him back every time because calls were monitored at his place of work, so he said, even though it was supposed to be his own company.

I had very fond memories of him. We had even considered marrying, but then I left the Midlands to attend university in London in 1968 and we lost contact. I always wondered if I'd made the right decision in marrying someone else, from whom I was subsequently divorced.

We met briefly in July 2002 – and what a shock! Here was this overweight, Skoda-driving financial advisor, who bore a very close resemblance to a bloated hamster, and clearly considered himself God's gift to all women.

Following this meeting, without any debate or discussion, he decided, during the course of one phone call, that because of his circumstances, he couldn't take the relationship any further. No debate, no discussion, that was that. I was left with a £284 mobile phone bill

Still, I look on the bright side: I *had* made the right decision 30 years ago to ditch this selfish apology for a man, and feel greatly comforted by the thought that he has been someone else's problem – not mine – for all this time! In my view, this was £284 very well spent.

Jenny Jones

Love And Death

I traced a cousin (Tryphena) whom I had not seen for 25 years last summer through FriendsReunited. My mother died in October and Tryphena came to the funeral. She was the third one to arrive at the crematorium: two other cousins, whom she hadn't seen for 25 years, were there before her. She and Andrew looked at each other and fell in love. They marry in September.

I've never known of anyone falling in love at a funeral.

Jennifer Airs, Sussex

Merry Christmas Everybody

Just want to tell you what happened at our school reunion back in November 2001.

I arrived at the club to find my very first girlfriend (from when I was six) standing there. She looked gorgeous.

We grew up through school, but didn't really speak. We then left school and went our different ways. I started work and totally lost touch for about 18 years, in which time she had had two long-term relationships and actually I had been married twice.

We chatted at the reunion all night, catching up on what we had been doing. I even found out that she had two pixies from the age of six that go on top of the Christmas tree each year and that they were named Hance and Jeanette (that's me and her). They go up every year and even her two partners knew them as that.

Isn't it spooky how it worked out? Because we are now living together and are planning on getting married in November and going on honeymoon to the Maldives!

Hance McGhie, Preston Grange, North Shields

TV

'Do you remember a show called *That's My Dog*? It was quite boring. I think it was presented by Derek Hobson. There was a maze in which the dogs got lost, the crap ones, that is. You'd think we were behind all that, but recently there was *Pets Win Prizes* with Dale Winton. What a cultural lot we are, eh?'

'I liked *Bullseye* with Jim Bowen, because the contestants used to win things like a fridge, or £70. But for how many years did I want a Dusty Bin from *3-2-1*? I tried to copy Ted Rogers' 3-2-1 fingers and never mastered it.'

'When I was younger, I used to watch *Tiswas*, where they "splatted" people with "custard pies". At the tender age of five, I believed that you would almost die, if you were "splatted" (because you'd suffocate) and felt so terrible for all these children and seventies celebs who were being terrorised. I had nightmares about being "splatted" for years after that.'

First Kiss

'I think my first kiss was in the mirror, practising for my first kiss. It was a bit flat, to tell you the truth.'

'One kiss that has stayed in my memory for all the wrong reasons was that of the first lad who tried to French kiss me. He hadn't quite got the technique and it was like being attacked by a cross between a washing machine and a vacuum cleaner. Euch! He also smelled of turpentine, since he was a decorator's apprentice. Lovely combination – spit and turps! Needless to say, we weren't together for very long.'

'I blush at the thought of my first kiss, I was about 13, I went out with an older lad. He walked me home, kissed me on the doorstep. He was taller than me, I snogged his chin. God I nearly died.'

'It was nasty. He was eating a Kit Kat and had it all around his mouth. It has put me off chocolate ever since.'

Loose Ends

Love, school, war — not all stories can be so neatly categorised, so before we go, here are some odds and ends. Amnesia, mountaineering, a goat, a medicine ball and a nasty case of 'Don't drink the water.' Something for everyone.

Memories

'I had a bad road accident at the end of 1998 with a brain injury that wiped out a lot of memories, hence using this site to re-learn. Love to hear from anyone that can tell me what I was like, good or bad, both would be useful and welcome. I've had a lot of replies to date and each one revives a memory that revives a further one for which I am grateful.'

This is part of my FriendsReunited member notes, which have generated some contact from others, who have helped in bringing back a significant proportion of my memory from my earlier years. I access the site very regularly and did so, in particular, at the early stages of this effort to assist my memory.

My head was previously 'just mush'. If you imagine that my memory was like a shed full of files, all cross-referenced and neatly stacked, and not a brick-built secure store but a very fragile building, then the accident was like a lorry crashing into the shed and sending the memories all over the place. Some were blown away, perhaps never to be seen again, others were partially destroyed, the remaining were in such a state of uproar that it was daunting beyond belief to start to reorganise.

I had one of those heads that was full of assorted rubbish and facts that you don't know are there until you are called upon to remember them in life. It could be a quiz question, or just a conversation with people you meet years down the line. I truly believed that we all had the same memory abilities and had no idea that my memory was what has been described since as 'exceptional'.

I could focus and recall things by replaying the incident or situation in my mind. This was particularly helpful in my work as an electrical engineer, when I needed to recall details of a property I worked in. If I thought I could not remember something that was critical to buying, or quoting after I returned home, rather than have to phone the customers, or return to site, I could play back the rooms or situations and that recall was accurate, even for sites from years earlier.

This memory loss caused me so much devastation after my accident. I was asleep for most of the first two months after the accident and was not aware of the problem until I started to be awake longer. I was then asked about the accident circumstances and had to re-read the written notes and commit them to memory. It didn't work at first, as there seemed to be a finite amount of 'working' memory available. As I started to return to work, this lack of ability to remember even small details was a major problem. Lots of trees had to come down to help me out! The amount of notes written at this time was phenomenal!

I went to my GP and was under a number of specialists for the brain injury and other effects of the accident. I became aware that the memory was 'noted' but no one was bothered about making efforts to help me re-learn.

That is why I welcomed FriendsReunited. I desperately needed a source of memories to re-organise my 'filing cabinets'. I was still experiencing problems reading then. I would read a paragraph and find that I had forgotten the beginning of it by the time I reached half way through.

Watching TV was a problem, as I could not keep up with who was who. The memory was therefore an obvious and major difficulty that required attention.

I started with FriendsReunited by contacting names that I felt I knew or should know. Sometimes the name gave me immediately a small burst of recall associated with that person. To their eternal credit, something of the order of 60–70 per cent replied. They would tell me some small thing they remembered about me or responded to the 'burst' of recall that I related and we were under way. Each little seed was planted and most took.

They each generated other recalls and we were soon making contact in groups, which maximised the chances of memory expansion.

It became apparent that my recall, even though 'damaged', was better than many of those I was contacting, as reported by them. This really encouraged me and lifted my spirits, essential when I was suffering severe depression after the accident, a lot of which was directly traceable to the daily frustration with my ability to recall.

At that time, I was getting lost driving a couple of villages away and did not recognise friends, places, or even remember the morning of the day I was on. This problem, funnily enough, remains. My long-term memory has dramatically improved. This has given me hope that, eventually, my recent memories of the last four and a half years since the accident may be there somewhere.

I contacted others on the back of others' memories and this has all contributed to my now having an almost crystal memory of when I was younger. There is no question that 'Without FriendsReunited, who knows?' is an apt way of putting the thanks forward

David Webster. Larkfield

Climb Every Mountain

For those of us who volunteered on those mountaineering school camps, 1976 was the year that men were men and sheep kept their distance.

Messrs Foster, Gilmore and others had done their usual perfect logistics exercise in transforming 30 odd of Parrenthorn High School's finest into promising Chris Bonnington look-a-likes.

Setting off from the school gates on a frosty, April morning, our hearts were set on conquering the peaks of Sca Fell Pike, Pillar, Steeple, and Great Gable, arriving at what looked like the end of the world by mid-afternoon; Wasdale, Cumbria.

Boys and girls (girls! well it wasn't all going to be doom and gloom ...) alike were housed in tents which were hopefully to become their home for what seemed to be the next ten years.

The following morning, as arranged, half of the group were to set off on a walk to Borrowdale via Sky-head Tarn. 'OK,' thinks me. 'I've got everything I need in my little rucksack, I'll go and report to Mr Gilmore.'

Big mistake, he modified my load with what seemed like the entire group's rations, a Himalayan sherpa would have pulled a face. As we set off the heavens opened, and opened, and opened. Looking back I'm sure Noah was pottering about on Wast Water Lake.

After fighting our way through the lashing storm, we arrived at Borrowdale campsite early evening.

Two thirds of the field were completely flooded, and like poor wretches we set about trying to erect our two-man tents on what grass was available. Freezing cold and wet through, to my dismay our tent didn't have a very important component: a pole. We managed a pathetic igloo and took shelter from the gale.

I received a request from Mr Foster for the rations I had been dragging around all day, which were in fact, a soaked sleeping bag, pooh!

David Hartley who was my co-pathetic tent lodger, kindly offered to take the rations to the teacher's tent (an excuse to get warm, if you ask me) and failed to return for some time.

It was a far better thing I did for my fellow man than allow myself to become a burden (© Captain Oates, North Pole). So, as the water level grew inside the tent, coming in through the hole where the pole should have been, I took David Hartley's sleeping bag and mopped it all up. Sorry David, but in doing this I then broke into howls of laughter, giggling mad, sadistic thoughts. (I think exposure was setting in.)

As the evening progressed, the water level rose up the field and one by one engulfed each tent.

For a time, all 16 of us were crammed into the teachers' four-man tent, each on our little perches. Come 4.00 a.m., we evacuated into the barn all huddled together in the hay, with the rats!

By daybreak, Mr Elmer had managed to navigate via the coast road (crashing the minibus on the way) with the help of Sid Sidieki to rescue the group and take us back to Wasdale campsite.

On arrival back, it was soon apparent that the campsite at Wasdale had not escaped the flood and I remember salvaging my soggy hold-all from the mess tent ... I was really miffed off by then.

But Mr Foster and Co pulled off the rental of a church hall in Strand, a few miles up the road, where the boys (and girls!) spent the week in each other's company sleeping on the floor of the hall.

That could have been the most horrendous episode of my life to date. But it didn't stop me going again the next year. Well, Janice Ainsley was going ...

All character building stuff!

Keith Jones, Whitefield, Manchester

Sailing

In 1959 I was 15 years old at school in Durban, South Africa, when my parents, after many years of saving, decided to take the holiday they had always dreamed of: a visit to the land of their ancestors, Britain! They had accumulated leave for many years and had a whole six months due and although they wanted to take 'the children' they felt it might be too long to keep us out of school. A colleague of my father had connections in Minehead, Somerset and it was decided that we should go to school there for three months and be billeted in the town.

In those days the usual way to travel, if you had the time, was on the Union Castle Line mail ship. I really dreamed of a wonderful cruise and shipboard romance but it didn't happen. At 15 I was too old for the children's activities and too young to attract the attention of all the handsome young men at the evening social events.

I ended up going to bed early most nights, upset at being a wallflower yet again. Then I would wake very early and go up on deck to watch the sun rise. Here I did attract the attention of a kindly Irish deckhand who felt sorry for this lonely little girl. His job, from 4 a.m. till 8 a.m., was to scrub the rails around the ship. I think if he had been scrubbing the deck we never would have talked but the rails were at a very sociable height and so began an unusual friendship. It was never a romance – I knew from the start that he was engaged.

When I was accepted into Minehead Grammar School I wrote to him care of the ship, mainly I think to boast that I had been considered clever enough to go to a grammar school. He never replied. Well, not for 43 years anyway and then – through FriendsReunited – he did!

Wendy Roy

The Great Escape

In Jefferson Road Secondary School (the Girls' side that is!) we used to keep animals including a goat! The ruddy thing got out (well, it was always escaping...), but this day it really went for it! It had the police and everybody out and managed to get half way across the Isle of Sheppey, causing chaos as it went, before it was rounded up and brought back to the school.

Across the town and half way up the island before being caught! We girls couldn't have done better!

Anon

Not Waving But Drowning

I was able to contact a school friend, who saved my life in 1985 and then moved away from my home town of Leeds in 1986.

I was drowning in one of the locks in the local canal after someone had opened the sluice gates and the force of the water and my weak arms sent me under. As I came back up all my friends who were with me were laughing hysterically and thought I was playing about as I was screaming.

Andrew looked in my eyes from the side and knew it was serious. As I was about to go under for the second time, he jumped in and dragged me away from the swell I was caught up in. We both knew that day that I owed him my life.

When we left school in 1986 Andrew left and moved to Blackpool with his family and I never heard from him again. At the beginning of last year I joined FriendsReunited and there Andrew was. I quickly joined and contacted him and thanked him for what he had done 15 years earlier.

Andrew told me he was about to get married and asked me to go up to Glasgow and be there for the day. I didn't need a second to make up my mind and travelled the 200 miles to be there for his big day. I was thrilled to be asked to do a reading from the Bible in the church. It was such a special day for us both, but more than anything it was my way of thanking him for saving my life that day.

Richard McCann

Bad Medicine

Let me set the picture: the fifth year boys of 1976 let loose in the gym unsupervised.

'I hope I can trust you to act sensibly and not use any gym equipment,' said our PE teacher, Mr Ken Webster. Mr Webster was the head of PE at the Holt. He had a permanent limp and a permanent frown.

We assembled in the gym like gladiators, waiting to do battle. Mr Webster started a game of Roman tag, was satisfied that it was running smoothly and then limped out of sight. Thirty seconds after his departure, gladiators we did in fact become. Using the most lethal of gladiator weapons, the medicine ball (and about ten of them), hastily extracted from the gym store, the mother of all battles ensued.

I could never figure out what medical benefit this ball could be used for, only the fact that if you ever tried to kick or head one, you would indeed require medicine in some form afterwards. It's slightly bigger than a normal sized football, normally covered in a brown heavy duty fabric and it is very heavy. It is used in gyms for weight training and stamina exercise for your stomach. You sometimes see boxers having them thrown at them.

Medicine balls were being used to 'attack' other boys. While my back was turned I was hit from behind with an accurate strike. Not wanting to miss out on the carnage, and seeking my revenge, I looked for a suitable target. I picked up a medicine ball and locked on to my intended victim. He was distracted, so I launched my medicine ball with every ounce of strength I could muster. I waited with bated breath, as my ball flew across the gym. Alas, I was not aware that my intended victim had the sight and speed of a peregrine falcon.

He ducked away with astounding agility. The medicine ball, however, was now travelling at the speed of sound and sailed gracefully over his head with a sonic boom. To my horror, its new target was now a gap between the wall bars and a supporting concrete pillar, protecting the enormous gym windows. I had unwittingly uncovered a serious design fault in the gym window protection system.

In ultra slow motion I watched as the supersonic missile continued on its way towards the biggest glass window in the school. It was like waiting for an atomic bomb to go off. And go off it certainly did. The loudest explosion of splintering glass I have ever witnessed erupted in front of me. In the confines of the gym it made the Hiroshima bomb sound like a popping champagne cork.

To my astonishment, there was an immediate end to gym hostilities and a graveyard silence of utter disbelief descended on the scene. I also witnessed the fastest clearing away of weapons of mass destruction back to the gym store that anyone could remember. As the culprit to this crime, I was singled out for every bit of sympathy 15-year-olds could bestow.

'Webo's goner kill yer' was reverberating round the shattered gym. I summoned up the courage to go and break the news to our beloved Mr Webster. I went to his room and knocked nervously on the door. Mr Webster's voice invited me in. I stood in front of his desk. 'Yes what is it?' he asked, annoyed.

'Sir, there has been an accident,' I said. 'Sir, I've just thrown a medicine ball through the gym window.'

I can't repeat what Mr Webster said, he being a father and family man too. He jumped up, barged past me and headed in the direction of the gym, as fast as he could limp. When he reached the gym he nearly took the doors off their hinges and he bellowed into the now silent amphitheatre for everyone to get into the changing rooms immediately.

Webo launched into his verbal attack. His ten-minute onslaught put Adolf Hitler and Fergie to shame. Boys were trying not to erupt into laughter. The slightest smile or titter detected by Webster would have resulted in certain crucifixion. He stopped suddenly. 'And where is the medicine ball?' he asked coldly, looking directly at me.

'It went through the window, Sir,' I managed to reply, with a straight face.

He looked around the changies and pointed at a boy who was in school uniform. He was one of the lucky ones not doing PE. The boy ran out instantly and returned, entering the changies like Clint Eastwood entering a saloon. He had everyone's attention. He proudly announced with glee: 'Sir, someone's robbed it!'

This was too much for everyone to take. The whole of the changing rooms erupted like Mount St Helens into uncontrollable laughter. Even Old Webo had a smile on his face. I never did find that medicine ball, although I am sure I saw Everton playing with it on *Match of the Day* a few weeks later.

Graham Leman, Poole, Dorset

Something In The Air

My husband Pete was in the RAF for 23 years and has been very ill for the past year. I decided to try and find a few of his friends for a reunion to cheer him up. After many, many hours of searching the site we are now only one week away from our reunion where there will be some 55 RAF footballers from all over the world enjoying a weekend of meeting lads they have not seen for 15–20 years or more. What can I say? A big thank you.

Lynne (Marilyn) Judge (née Williams)

Get Over It!

The saddest thing that happened to me at school was when I was pet monitor! I was about 13 years old. I lifted a gerbil out to clean the cage and its tail fell off. I was beside myself and sat in the toilets for about an hour! I had just got myself together, when the teacher told me that gerbils can't live alone, so the other one would die from loneliness. It did!

I still feel guilty to this day... 28 years later.

Anon

Bridge Over Troubled Water

June 1983

The suitcase had been long packed, the tickets sat on my dressing table, along with the Ambre Solaire and the hair crimper... Tenerife was just weeks away, two weeks of sunshine and romantic bliss. Just me and my boyfriend, whom we will call 'JH', and of course the other thousands of bodies crammed onto the greyish volcanic sands of the island. I couldn't wait!

July 1983

Disaster struck! On our way home from a night out at the Thames Court pub, JH told me the worst news I could have hoped to hear: we were finished, no more, no longer an item. Our names would have to be removed from the windscreen (or mine anyway); I was history! But the holiday we had booked together?

After much discussion and trauma at the travel agents, we found out that we were too late to return our pesetas and cancel the holiday without forfeiting our hard earned cash.

I was not looking forward to the prospect of two weeks on a lovely sunny island with a gorgeous boyfriend that no longer wanted me! With gritted teeth, I boarded the plane, and so the holiday began ...

JH's mum had asked me to 'look after' him whilst away and to ensure he didn't drink the water from the taps – he had to have lots of bottled mineral water. The first task when we got to our miniscule apartment, in which we had to spend 14 nights together, was to go shopping for water and other holiday paraphernalia. I purchased some more sun oil, and he the said water.

The next morning we had a particularly nasty and rather loud row, which most of the people waiting for the lift heard! I uttered expletives I never knew existed, but they were broadcast across most of Playa de las Americas ... Angrily, I stomped back to the apartment and in my fury, I saw the loathsome line-up of the mineral water. Something dark stirred in my mind and, with a gleeful smile, I walked towards them. I couldn't help it! My hands seemed to have disobeyed my conscience, and one by one by one, I tipped the crystal clear mineral water down the toilet.

Slowly, I walked to the bath and filled up every single bottle with the slighty murky water, screwed the tops back on and gave them a good shake to settle the 'bits' that came out of the tap. I carefully re-arranged them back in the kitchen, grabbed my coconut sun oil, Paul Young tape and hot-tailed it out to the beach.

Revenge was sweet! JH drank the water and, as I can recall, suffered an only minor (I think) bout of tummy upset, whilst I sat watching him drink the lot. The holiday droned on endlessly with us not speaking, going our separate ways both day and night.

2003

So, dear readers, that was that, you may think ... until 20 years later and the advent of a wonderful new website called FriendsReunited, where you could chat to old school friends, e-mail old work chums, even find a lonely heart or two ... But most of all, it gave me the opportunity to unburden myself of the 'Water Episode' guilt that had clung to me all those years and I gingerly typed in his name and waited ...

I found him, prepared my e-mail, held my breath and sent it!

Then I started to worry.

Would I have an e-mail back to say that he had been permanently affected by the bath water? Did he have irritable bowel syndrome? Had it discoloured his skin, or made his hair go green ...?

None of the above, dear readers. He did express some surprise as he had mistakenly thought I was a mild mannered little girl (apart from the swearing in the lift) and said that he had turned out into a mature happy man, despite this.

So the moral of the story? Yes, your past can come back to haunt you, but it's also now given me the opportunity to 'meet up' again after all these years, and we have found out about our lives and what we've done in those last two decades. We have exchanged photos and, although I no longer have the crimped hair and white handbag and stilettos, and he has finally thrown out his luminous pink-and-green socks, we have successfully emerged as two true friends reunited.

Julie Janes, Old Warden, Bedfordshire

The Truth Will Out

When I was twelve my father married a wonderful lady and took on her daughter who was six months my junior. For 15 years he made their lives hell, just the way he had with my family. But throughout, my stepsister and I grew to love and care for each other, comforting the pain either of us felt caused by my father.

Eight years ago, my lovely stepmother was struck down with cancer – she had never smoked a cigarette in her life but it literally choked her to death. Whilst she lay in bed at home, my father was having an affair with another woman in the very next room. Four days after she died he moved this other woman in and married her 10 months later. I wasn't allowed to go to my dear stepmother's funeral, to mention her name or to contact my stepsister again; I was told they had both hated me all along.

I was heartbroken; my stepsister and I had supported each other through thick and thin, pregnancies, births, marriages and divorces all before we were 20 years old and it hurt like a knife to think that she had hated me all that time.

A week ago I joined the FriendsReunited site and not only have I found many, many friends that I haven't seen for 17 years but I picked up the courage to e-mail my stepsister. I didn't think she would write back, but I had to tell her that I missed her so much. Twenty minutes later the phone rang and it was her; I was so shocked and guilty for the damage my father had done to her family that I couldn't speak at first. My stepsister calmed me down as she always could and called me back an hour later; the whole evening until 1 a.m. was spent phoning and e-mailing one another, and we both slept well that night.

I found out all the lies my father had told – and for the first time since she died I can speak my stepmum's name without sobbing. Thank you from the bottom of our hearts!

Anneliese

Closure

I found out my husband had a secret love child, a boy, who by this time was ten years old. I knew the mother of the child many years ago as she was an ex-girlfriend of my then boyfriend (husband).

Little did I know that after seven years of marriage and two children later they met up again and had an affair resulting in a son being born.

This dark secret was kept from me for the next ten years. I found out about it one night out with friends in a club. Well, you can imagine the shock I felt at the time. My husband and I had split up a few months before and when it was obvious to friends that I wasn't going to take him back, a lot of nasty secrets came out of the closet, so to speak.

Whatever he did throughout our marriage, nothing could have been worse than this. I knew this woman had emigrated to Australia, but hadn't a clue where.

Low and behold, I found her through the FriendsReunited website.

I made contact with her, as I had a good few things to get off of my chest. She did reply with the usual excuses (sorry etc), but all too late.

Anyway the point of the matter was, if it hadn't been for the FriendsReunited site, I would never have got to say how I felt, what I thought about their deceit and so on.

I would just like to say thanks for helping me to get my feelings out in the open through your site, and get on with the rest of my life.

Helen Wilson, Ayrshire

Honour Thy Mother

My mother, Mrs Una Angus was a teacher at the Lady Verney High School in High Wycombe. She is sadly no longer with us having died from cancer in 1989. From my point of view, and much more significantly from my father's, it has been heartwarming to read all the memories and kind words that have been placed on the site about my mum.

She obviously made an impact and even after all this time, it is so good to know that she was a happy memory for more than just her own immediate family. I guess in some ways she has been honoured in a way she would never have imagined.

Andy Angus

Some Friendly Facts

There are 56,849 schools registered, including one that is completely made up: Futlocks Remedial School. Some of the 'ex-pupils' include Nipples McGraw, Hugh Jorrifice, Humox O'Wilderbeast and Murdo McTurdie ... you get the picture. Jibbles Hemlock's notes include 'memories' of the school:

'Cleaning the Chemistry wing after one of Caulison Pealid's experiments had gone 'a bit wrong'. I'm not sure how many bodies I found that day. There were enough legs for about 15 pupils, but only enough arms for nine.'

As a result, there are 31,354 school reunions planned.

The school with the highest number of names registered for it is Crown Woods School, London with 5,631 members.

There are over 9,000,000 names registered on FriendsReunited, but sadly, 355,000 members have been deleted.

Some 353,000 photos have been placed on the site.

There are 506,408 work places registered.

There are 57,392 teams registered.

We send over 600,000 Christmas cards via the site each year.

There are 81 rude words on the banned word list (not including knickers).

Names

Not everybody wishes to use their real name when registering with
FriendsReunited. It's somewhat counter to the spirit of the site, but at the
same time your inalienable right to hide behind a pseudonym – some of
which are very popular indeed. Meanwhile others innocently share their
nomenclature with the rich and famous. Here's a roll call of those big names.

Names on the site	No.	Names on the site	No.
Jesus Christ	68	Elton John	18
John Smith	0,190	Cliff Richard	4
David Jones	2,007	David Bowie	20
David Beckham	115	Clark(e) Kent (Superman)	7
(many genuine)		Peter Parker (Spider-man)	110
Posh Spice	3	Michael Knight (*Knight Rider*)	129
Michael Owen	129	Mickey Mouse	369
Harry Potter (many genuine)	197	Minnie Mouse	80
Hugh Grant	18	Donald Duck	104
Julia Roberts	57	Adolf Hitler	98
Pamela Anderson	44	Fred West	18
Michael Douglas	68	Osama Bin Laden	325
(unfortunately, there are no		(under many spellings)	
Catherine Zeta-Jones)		Dennis the Menace	5
Elvis Presley	101		

Did you know that . . .

The first couple to marry as a result of meeting up on FriendsReunited was
Matt and Rae-Sarah Bascombe. They married in October 2001.

The 'oldest' reunion (that we know of) took place after the two people in
question, Jenny Rosen (née Nyman) and her friend had not seen each other
for around 80 years.

Since the website was launched, our Support Team have responded to over
2,000,000 e-mails from members.

There are also some spoof sites on the net of which Porn Stars Reunited and
Taliban Reunited are just two. Well, imitation is the sincerest form of flattery!

Epilogue

Do Look Back

Whether by luck or divine intervention, in October 2001 my own story – just one of those nine million – crossed paths with the FriendsReunited story. I heard about the site from my wife, who heard about it from her sister, and I registered without delay. I knew it was for me. I'd already appeared as a talking head on some of those nostalgia TV shows and saw no shame in dredging up the past.

By that time, I had become obsessed with miserable memoirs, books like Frank McCourt's *Angela's Ashes*, Dave Pelzer's *A Child Called 'It'*, Paul Morley's *Nothing*, and decided to pen my own. One problem: my childhood was free of trauma. Set in 1970s Northampton, my early history was free of death, divorce and deprivation: I got on well with my family, enjoyed school, played down the field, rode my bike, avoided hospital, discovered girls, kissed one or two of them, did my exams and left. To call it idyllic suggests that it was in some way special, but my theory is that most people live uneventful, ordinary childhoods. The stories in this book are often dramatic, tear-jerking, cinematic and life-changing, but they can't all be. Let's hear it for the rest of us.

Having decided that a book about nothing much happening in a provincial town in the seventies might just find an audience, FriendsReunited entered my life like a shaft of light. Of course! Reunite with friends! Reconnect with my past and ratify through others that it really was as mundane and yet profound as I remembered it! I signed up – unaware that membership had just tipped two million – in the familiar hope of finding some of my old school pals and dipping a toe in the past. I revealed in my FriendsReunited entry that I was researching this book and encouraged anyone who knew me to get in touch.

They did.

Anita first, then Craig McKenna, Paul Milner, Paul Bush, Alan Martin, Dave Griffiths, Kevin Pearce, Wendy Turner, Lis Ribbans, Ricky Hennell, Mark Crilley, Jo Flanders, Chris Dashfield, Andy Howkins, Jackie Needham, Neil Meadows — I list them all because, although they might appear to be just a bunch of names, to me they represent an all-star cast. And that's why FriendsReunited is so unique. It makes us all important.

We shared our childhood memories via e-mail over the coming months. I ran my own memories past some of the people involved (Anita still maintains that she doesn't remember me putting my arm around her while she was going out with Paul Bush!); I made sure that nobody minded little glimpses of their lives being put into print (especially those who grew up to be men or women of the cloth!); and in the case of Alan Martin — now living in New Zealand — I ran an entire, rather more controversial chapter past him for libel (he gave it the thumbs up). To say that I couldn't have written my book without FriendsReunited is not to overstate the case.

Of course, you don't have to be preparing your memoirs to profit from the site: the fountain of the past is for all to sup at. Never mind the old flames, the lost sons, the childhood sweethearts walking up the aisle and having babies — it's just as important as a way of saying 'hi', finding out that Chris, whose mum had the Soda Stream, now works in IT and has two lovely daughters.

After the publication of my book, FriendsReunited really came into its own. People are still using the site as a means of getting in touch — and I mean people I've never met. FriendsReunited does more than simply reunite. Sometimes it just unites.

Having expanded into Ireland, Australia, Italy, Spain, South Africa, the Netherlands, New Zealand and Germany, it's tempting to say, 'Tomorrow, the world!' (That's certainly what the new chief executives are saying.) But FriendsReunited's expansion across the oceans is no real surprise. As an idea it was always going to translate abroad. The past may not be a foreign country, but every foreign country has a past.

We need not fear the implications of all this growth. FriendsReunited is as big as the database and yet as intimate as that first e-mail. Compilation CDs, books and live music events may be 'brand extensions' in the eyes of marketing folk, but these always link back to the site, whether members are being polled for track listings, or asked for stories to form the basis of a book like this one. Moves into Sky Digital and mobile phones will only make the site more accessible. The proposed FriendsReunited Lottery has all the hallmarks of a Steve and Julie idea – you choose the charities where you want your ticket money to end up, and nobody else makes any profit. Richard Branson would be proud of them.

FriendsReunited may still strike some cynics as sad: a hunch of deluded souls unable to connect with the present, wallowing pointlessly in the past but we know it's not like that. Nor is it a simple case of achieving what the Americans call 'closure'. Our lives are full of unfinished business, truths unspoken, problems unresolved, and FriendsReunited allows us to go back and tidy up. It's a form of liberation.

The name Pankhurst was for the best part of a century shorthand for emancipation, thanks to Emmeline and her daughters Sylvia and Christabel, whose tireless, often dangerous work led to women's suffrage. Steve and Julie Pankhurst might not feel they are fighting any kind of political fight, or indeed making history, but from where I'm sitting, simply by not selling out they are doing both.

From equal voting rights for women to equal reminiscing rights for everybody. It's a short walk to freedom after all, and still only the price of a couple of drinks. Long may the soap opera continue.

Andrew Collins, London